SIERRA CLUB EXHIBIT FORMAT SERIES

Winner of the Carey-Thomas Award in 1964
  for the best achievement in creative publishing in the United States

EDITED BY DAVID BROWER

THE EARTH'S WILD PLACES

within the Exhibit Format Series, a special series on
wildness around the world, published in cooperation with
The Conservation Foundation

And when both Seas and Lands have compast been
Ther's some thing still unfound, some thing unseen.

—MILDMAY FANE 1640

GALÁPAGOS: THE FLOW OF WILDNESS

I. DISCOVERY

Puerto Viejo, April 26, 1535.

Sacred Imperial Catholic Majesty:

It seemed right to me to let Your Majesty know the progress of my
trip from the time when I left Panama, which was on the twenty-third of
February of the current year, until I arrived in this new town of Puerto Viejo.

The ship sailed with very good breezes for seven days, and the pilot
kept near land and we had a six-day calm; the currents were so strong
and engulfed us in such a way that on Wednesday, the tenth of March,
we sighted an island; and, as on board there was enough water for only two
more days, they agreed to lower the life-boat and go on land for water
and grass for the horses, and once out, they found nothing but seals,
and turtles, and such big tortoises, that each could carry a man on top
of itself, and many iguanas that are like serpents.

On another day, we saw another island larger than the first, and with
great sierras; and thinking that on account of its size and monstrous shape,
there could not fail to be rivers and fruits, we went to it, because the
distance around the first one was about four or five leagues and around
the other, ten or twelve leagues, and at this juncture the water on the ship
gave out and we were three days in reaching the island on account of the
calms, during which all of us, as well as the horses, suffered great hardships.

. . .

The boat once anchored, we all went on land, and some were given charge
of making a well, and others looking for water over the island;
from the well there came out water saltier than that of the sea; on land
they were not able to find even a drop of water for two days and with the
thirst the people felt they resorted to a leaf of some thistles like
prickly pears, and because they were somewhat juicy, although not very
tasty, we began to eat of them and squeeze them to draw all the water
from them, and drawn, it looked like slops, or lye, and they drank
of it as if it were rose water.

. . .

On Passion Sunday, I had them bring on land the things necessary for saying Mass, and after it was said, I again sent the people in twos and threes, over different parts. The Lord deigned that they should find in a ravine among the rocks as much as a hogshead of water, and after they had drawn that, they found more and more. In fine, eight hogsheads were filled and the barrels and the jugs that there were on the boat, but through the lack of water we lost one man and two days after we left the island we lost another; and ten horses died.

. . .

From this island we saw two others, one much larger than all, which was
easily fifteen or twenty leagues around; the other was medium; I took
the latitude to know where the islands were and they are between
half a degree and a degree and a half south latitude. On this second one,
the same conditions prevailed as on the first; many seals, turtles, iguanas,
tortoises, many birds like those of Spain, but so silly they do not know
how to flee, and many were caught in the hand. The other two islands
we did not touch; I do not know their character. On this one, on the sands
of the shore, there were small stones, that we stepped on as we landed,
and they were diamond-like stones and others amber colored; but on
this whole island, I do not think that there is a place where one might sow
a bushel of corn, because most of it is full of very big stones, so much so,
that it seems as though some time God had showered stones; and the
earth that there is, is like dross, worthless, because it has not the power
of raising a little grass.

. . .

Thinking that we were not more than twenty or thirty leagues from this soil of Peru, we were satisfied with the water already mentioned, although we might have filled more of our casks; but we set sail, and with medium weather we sailed eleven days without sighting land, and the pilot and the master of the ship came to me to ask me where we were and to tell me there was only one hogshead of water on the ship. I tried to take the altitude of the sun that day and found that we were three degrees south latitude, and I realized that with the direction we were taking, we were becoming more and more engulfed, that we were not even heading for land, because we were sailing south; I had them tack on the other side, and the hogshead of water I had divided as follows: half was given for the animals, and with the other half a beverage was made which was put into the wine cask, for I held it as certain that we could not be far from land, and we sailed for eight days, all of which the hogshead of the beverage lasted, by giving a ration to each one with which he was satisfied. And when the hogshead gave out and there was no relief for us, we sighted land and we had calm for two days, during which we drank only wine, but we took heart on sighting land. We entered the bay and river of the Caraques on Friday, the ninth of April, and we met there the people of the galleon from Nicaragua, who had left Nicaragua eight months before, so we considered our trip good in comparison with theirs. . . .

—The Lord fill Your Sacred Majesty with holy love and grace for many years and with the conservation of your realms and an increase of other new ones as I hope. From this new town of Puerto Viejo, the twenty-sixth of April, in the year fifteen hundred and thirty-five. I am Your Sacred Imperial Catholic Majesty's most true servant and subject and perpetual Chaplain who kisses your royal feet and hands.

—Fray Tomás eps. Locastelli Auril

Marine iguana, Hood Island

*Considering the small size of these islands, we feel the more astonished
at the number of their aboriginal beings, and at their confined range.
Seeing every height crowned with its crater, and the boundaries of
most of the lava-streams still distinct, we are led to believe
that within a period, geologically recent, the unbroken ocean
was here spread out. Hence, both in space and time, we seem to be brought
somewhat near to that great fact—that mystery of mysteries—
the first appearance of new beings on earth.*

CHARLES DARWIN

1. *Discovery*

photographs by Eliot Porter

introduction by Loren Eiseley,

*with selections from Herman Melville, Charles Darwin,
J. R. Slevin, William Beebe, and others*

edited by Kenneth Brower

foreword by David Brower

GALAPAGOS

The Flow of Wildness

SIERRA CLUB   SAN FRANCISCO · NEW YORK · LONDON

Publisher's note: The book is set in Centaur and Arrighi by Mackenzie & Harris,
Inc., San Francisco, with assistance from Sun Engraving, 6-10 Kirby Street, London.
The color separations and films are by Carl de Schutter, Antwerp. The book is
lithographed on Star Astralux by Garrod & Lofthouse Ltd., London, and
double-spread collated and bound in Winterbottom's Art Canvas by Webb Son & Co.
Ltd., London. The design is by David Brower.

We are grateful for permission to reprint excerpts from these books:
California Academy of Sciences, San Francisco: "Log of the Schooner
'Academy' on a Voyage of Scientific Research to the Galapagos Islands,
1905-1906," by J. R. Slevin, *The Occasional Papers of the California Academy of Sciences,*
copyright 1931.
The Oxford University Press, New York: *Ecuador the Unknown,* by Victor
Wolfgang Von Hagen, copyright 1940.
G. P. Putnam's Sons, New York: *Galapagos: World's End,* by William Beebe,
copyright 1924.
G. P. Putnam's Sons, New York: *The Arcturus Adventure,* by William Beebe,
copyright 1926.

Library of Congress Catalog Card Number 68-54319

The Sierra Club, founded in 1892 by John Muir, has devoted itself
to the study and protection of scenic resources and wild places around
the world. Sierra Club publications are part of the nonprofit effort
the club carries on as a public trust. The club is affiliated with the
International Union for Conservation, the National Resources Council
of America, and the Federation of Western Outdoor Clubs. There
are chapters in California, the Pacific Northwest, The Great Basin, the
Southwest, The Great Lakes region, and on the Atlantic seaboard.
Participation is invited in the program to enjoy and preserve wilderness,
wildlife, forests and streams. Main office: Mills Tower, San Francisco.
Other offices: 15 East 53rd Street, New York: 235 Massachusetts
Avenue, N.E., Washington, D.C.; Auditorium Building, Los Angeles;
6 Langley Street, London WC2.

Printed in England.

PUBLISHED IN COÖPERATION WITH THE CONSERVATION FOUNDATION

CONTENTS

SIXTY-NINE COLOR PLATES

Miguel Cabello de Balboa, en 1586 en su libro "Miscelanea Austral" y Pedro Sarmiento de Gamboa, en 1572, en su "Historia de los Incas," relatan el extraordinario viaje del Inca Tupac Yupanqui (abuelo del Inca Quiteño: Atahualpa) a unas Islas perdidas, allá, lejos, muy lejos, en medio de la Mama Cocha o Madre de las Lagunas, como traduce el primer cronista, que de regreso trajo "muchos prisioneros de piel negra, mucho oro y plata, un trono de cobre y pieles semejantes a los caballos." Y Sarmiento, en su relato similar anota que dichos "trofeos se guardaron en la fortaleza del Cuzco hasta el tiempo de los españoles." Unico Inca navegante, el décimo de su dinastía bautizó a dos islas: Hahua-Chumbi, la isla de Afuera y Nina Chumbi, la isla de Fuego (quizas porque fue testigo de una erupción volcánica) según ambas crónicas recogidas de labios de ancianos indios cuzqueños. Así, las balsas de los Mantas y de los Punaes habían realizado la hazaña de ensanchar el Imperio del Tahuantinsuyu del ambicioso y valiente conquistador. Y esto sucedía en medio del Pacífico y a mediados del siglo quince.

Casi cien años despues, una carta del 26 de Abril de 1535, dirigida al Emperador de las Españas, Carlos Quinto, por el fray dominicano Tomás de Berlanga, Obispo de Castilla de Oro (como se llamaba en aquel entonces a Panamá), relata su naufragio sobre unas islas desiertas, solo pobladas de "lobos marinos, tortugas, iguanas y galápagos," que desaparecían frecuentemente entre las nieblas y a las cuales bautizó cristiana y castellanamente: Las Islas Encantadas.

Aquello sucedía apenas a los 43 años de la llegada de las carabelas españolas al nuevo continente, 22 despues del descubrimiento del Mar del Sur, por Vasco Nuñez de Balboa y escasamente a los cuatro meses de la fundación de la Muy Noble y Muy Leal Cuidad de San Francisco de Quito, perdida en el altiplano andino. Era la primera noticia sobre las islas Galápagos para el mundo civilizado del Renacimiento europeo.

Despues, pasaron corsarios y balleneros, científicos y escritores, conquistando cada cual, oro, cachalotes o odeas. La larga lista ha jalonado las islas y la historia de hispano américa. La teoría de la evolución nació allí, quizas debido a la observación acuciosa del vice gobernador, héroe de la independencia de Guayaquil, José de Villamil, hecha a Darwin, mostrándole las diferencias entre los galápagos provenientes de distintas islas, como lo anotó el sabio inglés en su libro. Villamil, nació en Louisiana, de padre español y madre francesa, como para mostrar que, en Galápagos, se sintetizan las razas y las ideas, para asi destacarse mejor sobre el horizonte mundial.

Pero, en nuestros días, a los cuatrocientos años del viaje del Inca, son los fotógrafos, los nuevos conquistadores de la imagen y del colorido de esos paisajes salvajes, áridos y prehistóricos que nos emocionan con sus maravillas gráficas. Y No solamente son pictóricas, sino que muchas veces nos hacen vibrar al unísono de las ignoradas pasiones de animales raros, en sus luchas y amores; o, como el geyser del volcan Alcedo, nos hace pensar en el aliento casi hirviendo de nuestro planeta, que ha escogido, —quizas por verguenza,—ese lugar escondido y solitario, para desfogar su resuello pútrido y caliente.

Mi amigo admirado, Eliot Porter examina, calcula y pule, con el corazón, cada una de sus vistas, tal cual hizo el poeta José María de Heredia, en sus sonetos, cuando habla del mundo hispano americano o de los sueños ignotos de los Conquistadores. Y, asi consigue que cada uno de sus cuadros sea también un soneto de luces y de imágenes, verdadero poema visual de la naturaleza que nuestros débiles ojos no han sido capaces de admirar.

Viendolo escoger friamente sus temas entre las coloniales esculturas de madera, bajo los claustros franciscanos (fundados por un "pariente cercano" de Carlos Quinto) en el museo de esta ciudad, pensé en la superioridad del artista, pero nunca pude imaginarme que esos ojos traducían en versos brillantes de luces, formas y contrastes, el alma del hombre pacífico, ante las incomparables bellezas de la naturaleza.

Gracias, señores del Sierra Club, de la villa homónima y hermana de la mía, por sus delicados sentimientos semejantes a los del Santo Seráfico de Asis, del cual ambas llevan el glorioso nombre; gracias mil. Han sabido ustedes comprender la colaboración internacional al apreciar un sector de mi Patria, para embellecerlo, ponerlo de relieve y presentarlo tan elegantemente al publico del mundo.

Y para los lectores, que el corto momento de admiración dedicado a esas fotografías únicas, sea, también, un bálsamo de dulzura, de poesía y de confraternidad, en medio del diario bregar por la vida. Y, que esa confraternidad nos ayude a nosotros los ecuatorianos, a defender y conservar esas bellezas en su habitat natural y agreste, para que las futuras generaciones puedan, con mejores facilidades, contemplarlas; ensayando de superar, —probablemente sin lograrlo,— los motivos y las emociones que presentan estos soberbios libros de arte.

CRISTÓBAL BONIFAZ JIJÓN

San Francisco de Quito,
a 10 de Agosto de 1968, Fiesta Nacional del Ecuador y Aniversario
del Primer Grito de la Independencia de Hispano América.

Miguel Cabello de Balboa in 1586 in his book *Miscelanea Austral* and Pedro Sarmiento de Gamboa in 1572 in his *Historia de los Incas* relate the extraordinary voyage of the Inca Tupac Yupanqui (grandfather of the Quito Inca, Atahualpa) to some lost islands very, very far away in the middle of Mama Cocha, or Mother of the Lagoons, as Cabello translates. On his return he brought "many black-skinned prisoners, much gold and silver, a copper throne, and hides similar to cow hides." Sarmiento in his similar account notes that "these trophies were guarded in the fortress at Cuzco until the time of the Spaniards." The Inca, the tenth of his dynasty, named the two islands Hahua-Chumbi, the outer island, and Nina-Chumbi, the island of fire (perhaps because he had witnessed a volcanic eruption) according to both chronicles, which had been recorded from the lips of the old men of Cuzco. Thus, halfway through the fifteenth century, the balsas of the peoples of Manta and Puná had accomplished the feat of extending the ambitious and valiant conqueror's empire of Tahuantinsuyu to the middle of the Pacific.

Almost one hundred years later, a letter dated 26 April 1535, addressed to the Emperor of the Spains, Charles V, by the Dominican monk Tomás de Berlanga, Bishop of Castilla de Oro (as Panama was called at that time) relates his shipwreck on some deserted islands populated only by sea lions, turtles, iguanas, and tortoises, islands that frequently disappeared into the fog. In a way both Christian and Spanish he baptized them The Enchanted Islands.

That happened scarcely forty-three years after the arrival of the Spanish caravels at the new continent, twenty-two years after the discovery of the Southern Sea by Vasco Nuñez de Balboa and just four months after the founding of the very noble and very loyal city of San Francisco de Quito, hidden in the Andean altiplano. It was the first awareness that the civilized world of Renaissance Europe had of the Galápagos Islands. Later, pirates, whalers, scientists, and writers passed by, each winning gold, whales, or ideas, and the long list of voyagers has charted the islands. The theory of evolution was born there, perhaps aided by the astute observation which the Vice-Governor José de Villamil, hero of Guayaquil independence, made to Darwin, showing him the differences among the tortoises native to separate islands, an observation the English scholar noted in his book. Villamil was born in Louisiana of a Spanish father and a French mother, as if to show that in the Galápagos races and ideas are always synthesized so as to stand out better on the world horizon.

But in our time, four hundred years after the Inca's voyage, come the new conquerors of the shape and color of those untamed, arid, and prehistoric landscapes—the photographers, who stir us with their marvelous pictures. What we feel is not only visual, for often we are made to vibrate in unison with unknown passions of rare animals in their conflicts and their loves; or the eruption of the Alcedo volcano makes us think about the seething of our planet that has chosen perhaps through shame that solitary and out-of-the-way place to exhale its hot and putrid breath.

My esteemed friend, Eliot Porter, examines, calculates and polishes—from his heart—each thing his camera sights just as the poet José María de Heredia did in his sonnets when he speaks of the Spanish American world or of the unknown dreams of the Conquistadores. And so each one of his pictures is also a sonnet of lights and images, a true visual poem of the nature which our weak eyes have not been capable of admiring.

Watching him coolly selecting his themes among the wooden colonial structures, beneath the Franciscan cloisters (founded by a "close relative" of Charles V) in the museum of this city, I thought about the superiority of the artist, but I never could imagine that those eyes would translate into brilliant verses of light, shapes and contrasts, the soul of the pacific man before the incomparable beauties of Nature.

Thank you, gentlemen of the Sierra Club, from the town of the same name which is my sister-town, for your delicate sentiments so like those of the Saint of Assisi from whom both bear the glorious name—a thousand thanks. You have understood international collaboration in appreciating a part of my country in order to beautify it, put it in a place of prominence and present it so elegantly before the public of the world.

And for the readers I hope that the brief moment of admiration dedicated to these unique photographs will also be a balm of sweetness, poetry, and brotherhood in the midst of the daily struggle for life. And I trust that this brotherhood will help us Ecuadorians to protect and conserve that beauty in its natural and untamed habitat so that future generations may, with greater facility, contemplate them, trying to excel—probably without succeeding—the motives and the emotions which present these superb books of art.

CRISTÓBAL BONIFAZ JIJÓN

San Francisco de Quito,
10 August 1968, National Feast of Ecuador and Anniversary of the first cry of independence in Spanish America.

When we try to pick out anything by itself, we find it hitched to everything else in the universe. —JOHN MUIR

Thirty-one years after his birth in a Scottish town on the North Sea, John Muir was exploring the High Sierra, still one of the most impressive of the earth's wild places, and was learning, with Henry David Thoreau, that in wildness is the preservation of the world.

The Sierra Club, founded in 1892 by Muir, shares the insight of both men with many organizations devoted to preservation of the earth's remaining vestige of wildness. Muir put together a small mountain club whose members were primarily concerned with the Sierra Nevada. But he would realize why that concern must be broadened; ecologist, mountain traveler, inventor, and writer, he knew about the interrelatedness of things; he knew that if wilderness were being plundered in one land, it would be imperiled in another; he knew about the strength that would come to the defenders of wildness if they joined together; he knew that in that wildness there was a flow, a continuum, a refining of an evolutionary force that had succeeded too well to be obliterated, either intentionally or carelessly, by man, one of evolution's many notable successes.

Muir would have hailed the Sierra Club's Galápagos venture and what it can surely lead to. Eliot Porter, whose idea the venture was, long ago discovered, in trying to photograph some detail by itself, that it was indeed hitched to other things in the universe. His photographs speak of the wholeness of things. Seven volumes the size of these now testify to his perception, to the force of his seeing, and to the contagion of it. Those parts of the earth's wild places that have known his lens are fortunate. May there be many more!

The editor of the present volumes, Kenneth Brower, has explained their purpose:

" 'Voyages without islands to touch upon would be epics of monotony,' Loren Eiseley writes in his Introduction to these volumes. 'Whether for diversion of thought or for the easing of the physical body, men demand mental periods, points of reference, islands fixed in the turbulence of giant waters, or, if eluding the compass, still haunting the mind. . . .'

"This is a book in praise of islands. Its two volumes are an investigation of the virtues of islands as points of reference, both scientific and poetic. They are concerned with islands as laboratories, refuges, genetic reservoirs, places for future discovery. The book arose from concern for islands and the fragile life forms they have evolved, the gentle insular wildness that is vanishing so rapidly around the world. Its concern is both for oceanic islands like the Galápagos, and for islands isolated in other ways—for islands of life, like the very small North American island of whooping cranes, a last island of common genes and nesting calls, or like the limited fraternity of the Indian rhinoceros, or that of the freshwater seals of Lake Baikal. Its plea is for diversity, for all possible variety, animate and inanimate, in the texture of our planet's surface.

"There is a sign in the Bronx Zoo that is to the point, and whoever wrote it understood the need for this book. 'This red symbol,' the sign reads, 'calls attention to endangered species. Look for it around the Bronx Zoo. And think about what it means—the final emptiness of extinction.' We don't need more emptiness in the world—there is presently a surfeit of that. We need to celebrate the opposite of emptiness, and this book is the first in a series that will attempt to do this, to point out the fullness and variousness of the earth's wild places.

"A living planet is a rare thing, perhaps the rarest in the universe, and a very tenuous experiment at best. We need all the company we can get on our unlikely journey. If an island is washed away mankind is the less: One species' death diminishes us, for we are involved in life. The more varied the life the better. There is no requirement that our voyage be a monotonous one."

The scope of the volumes grew, and two other organizations materially helped this come about—The Conservation Foundation and the Nature Conservancy. Dr. Maria Buchinger is head of the Conservancy's Latinamerican Division, and John Milton, who was a member of the Galápagos expedition, is head of the Foundation's office of International Studies. In 'Man and the Land in Ecuador" (*Sierra Club Bulletin,* October 1967) he and Dr. Buchinger describe a threat few were aware of when the project began:

"The United States and other highly developed countries have been spending vast sums on widely varied foreign assistance, all too often motivated by short-range economic criteria and giving little consideration to social, ecological, aesthetic, and long-range economic impacts of development projects.

"Greatly expanded efforts will be needed to counteract successfully the adverse effects of much of our own country's massive governmental and private 'development' programs throughout the world. We hope more North Americans will take heed of environmental problems in developing nations like Ecuador. At best this will lead to an accelerated support of local conservation activities—in Ecuador and wherever similar local efforts exist in the 'underdeveloped' world. Moreover, in the excitement of watching our own technology change the face of our part of the Americas, we have overlooked some important lessons abroad. Increased contact with other countries like Ecuador will often permit us to learn from those who have already worked out an enduring relationship with the land. The 'underdeveloped world' has much to teach us.''

I believe that the earth man has already touched—sometimes gently and sometimes brutally—can sustain his advancing civilization if he applies his science, his technology, and his genius to the challenge of going back over what he has touched and ameliorating his mistakes. Hardly a tenth of that earth is still essentially uninterrupted by his technology. This is the wilderness, an increasingly rare thing that civilization's old patterns of growth can overrun swiftly, but to little avail. Man can tear the miracle of wilderness apart but he cannot reassemble it, and the vestige that too few people know about is all that men will ever have. It contains answers to questions man has not yet learned how to ask.

Man is prolific enough to explode across the land, but he can only do so at the expense of the organic diversity essential to the only world he can live upon. When beaver populations explode, the beaver overload their range, become neurotic, lose vitality, and starve. Mankind has a range, too, and it has a maximum carrying capacity consistent with a good life—a life with enough resources on hand to serve a restrained population and to spare nations from a final quarrel over them.

Man needs an Earth International Park, to protect on this planet what he has not destroyed and what need not be destroyed. In this action, all the nations could unite against the one real common enemy—Rampant Technology. Here might be rescued, for the improved men we should hope will be born in centuries and millenia to come, the natural places where answers can always be sought to questions man may one day be wise enough to ask.

We hope the Galápagos volumes will be prologue to a series of books on the earth's wild places in which the Conservation Foundation, the Sierra Club, The World Wildlife Fund, the International Union for the Conservation of Nature, and other organizations sharing their purpose can work together. They need to do so in time, mindful of what Adlai Stevenson said: "We travel together, passengers on a little space ship, dependant on its vulnerable reserves of air and soil; all committed for our safety to its security and peace; preserved from annihilation only by the care, the work and, I will say, the love we give our fragile craft.''

*   *   *

It is a pleasant and alarming task to wind up five years' effort by acknowledging the work of those who made it possible—pleasant in whom you remember and alarming in whom you forget.

First, we are deeply grateful to Eliot Porter. Five years ago, with his "*In Wildness*" just beginning its great success, he told us of his interest in photographing in the Galápagos Islands; he sought foundation help for the necessary expedition, suggesting that the Sierra Club was the likely publisher. Some club officials did not then think the equator was close enough to the club's interests, but others did. A series of steps began, each of which would have to succeed or the project would not. Dr. Harold J. Coolidge, of the Pacific Science Institute and a moving force in international conservation, arranged for a presentation of the idea at the 1963 annual meeting of the Darwin Foundation. Another expedition was about to get started, and fear was expressed that adding Sierra Club participants might complicate things—as one man expressed it, produce too many Galápagos books. The Darwin Foundation thought differently and encouraged our plan; but the club could not yet give financial help, and much help would be needed if the club had to organize a separate expedition. Things looked dim and a majority of the Publications Committee voted to abandon the project. Others, however, felt differently, especially those who were becoming impressed with what the club publications were doing in the conservation world. John Milton and Maria Buchinger were among them. Assuming that the plans would in good time succeed, they urged that the club could help by bringing two Ecuadorians to the University of Michigan for a seminar on national park administration. A generous (and anonymous) grant to the club made this possible and a series of meetings began that progressively aided the prospects of an expedition and the likelihood of its success.

The financial barrier persisted until Eliot Porter was able to lend the club enough to cover most of the expedition costs, with repayment contingent upon the success of a book based on the expedition. Half as much again was added from two small club funds at my discretion, and the expedition departed in February 1966, its planning assisted by Professor Robert L. Usinger of the University of California, Berkeley; Dr. Allan Cox, of the U.S. Geological Survey; and Frank Masland, a supporter of the Darwin Foundation's program. Robert V. Golden, veteran of many Sierra Club outings, helped gather men and goods, pledging a large block of his personal stock to ease the expedition out of Customs difficulties.

In Quito and Guayaquil help came from many sources. Cristobal Bonifaz Jijon of Quito, who has written our preface, also provided endless courtesies and rescues from culture shock. The support of the Ecuadorian government was invaluable. We are especially grateful to Ingeniero Teodoro Suarez, chief of Forest Management, and to Dr. Misael Acosta-Solis, founder of the Ecuadorian Institute of Natural Sciences.

We thank the members of the expedition whose names do not appear on the title page; Steve and Kathy Porter, Tad and Mary Jane Nichols. We are deeply indebted to the people of the Galápagos whose help and hospitality made the Islands less an archipelago of aridities for the expedition: to Gusch, Carl, and Fritz Angermeyer and their wives; to Fiddi Angermeyer; to Miguel Castro, Dr. Roger Perry, and the Darwin Station staff; to Marlena and Clara Paredes and Aurora Andrare; to Mr. and Mrs. Edgar Pots and Mr. and Mrs. Horneman. We are grateful to Forrest Nelson, José Luis, and their Galápagos radio, to Marie Laub and her California radio, for keeping the expedition in touch with the mainland of two Americas.

Loren Eiseley unhappily could not go on the expedition itself, but agreed to introduce the book, letting Eliot Porter's eyes substitute for his own, augmenting this view, as only Dr. Eiseley could, with a unique understanding of what islands mean to man, especially these islands.

Eliot Porter did not fail him. He did, however, perplex us by photographing so well that we needed two volumes, each quite costly to produce. But the club's commitment to get the books out somehow was clear, and as W. H. Murray said, "The moment one definitely commits oneself, then Providence moves too. All sorts of things occur to help one that would never otherwise have occurred. A whole stream of events issues from the decision . . ." One such event, aided by our Southwest man, Jeffrey Ingram, was an anonymous gift, "a contribution of securities valued at approximately sixty-five thousand dollars that are required to be expended in England . . . We should like the fund initially to support the Galápagos volumes. To such extent as they subsequently succeed financially, we should like the fund to be reimbursed and applied to subsequent volumes in the series that serve the same purpose—to inform the public about various endangered islands of wilderness elsewhere in the world."

Now we could move more rapidly in this, the club's boldest publishing venture. The Conservation Foundation and especially Judge Russell Train, its president, added to the cooperation we had already enjoyed when he contributed John Milton's talent and energy to our joint effort. Protection of a worldwide wilderness heritage was not to be just a one-time thing, but an involvement of the best thinking of both organizations and their many friends. Among these, special thanks are quite easy to extend because they go to another editor, my wife, who not only gave encouragement and reencouragement throughout the slow gestation of the books, but was also chief architect of the editor of the two volumes, who already knows more about what should go in Exhibit Format books than his father did. His participation in the expedition was rewarding.

A most pleasant task was finding out how to use the club's blocked Sterling gift. Hugh Barnes, who lithographed much of the club's color work in New York, did the initial searching for an English printer, and in October 1967 we were watching a handsome color test sheet come off press at the Garrod and Lofthouse works in Crawley, just south of London. Ground rules were written for the Great Trans-Atlantic Printing Match, in which one sixteen-page color form would be run on similar presses in both New York and London from identical color separations. Norman Garrod's people, especially Rivers Royston, helped in many ways. A London office of the club was established in Covent Garden and a new entity, Sierra Club Limited, was chartered, with an official address in Pall Mall, just about 350 miles south of John Muir's birthplace.

So there you have it—a book written by Spanish sailors, English pirates, Yankee whalers, and scientists from all over; a book published with the help of the Ecuadorian government by a North American club founded by a Scotsman and printed in England from color separations made in Belgium, all of it to affect whoever now cares, or should, that wildness not cease flowing on the planet we can remain aboard only as long as the flow goes on.

The final acknowledgment, then, is the important one: to all who take the idea to which these volumes are prologue, who add their own creative thought, clarify the idea, and see that it succeeds.

DAVID BROWER
Executive Director, Sierra Club

London, July 21, 1968

INTRODUCTION

ROCK REDONDO: Science and Literature in the Galápagos

"We sailed away to the Westward to see if we could find those Islands called the Galipoloes," recorded Edward Davis, a buccaneer captain, in 1684. The Spaniards had laughed provokingly, telling the English freebooters that what they sought were "Inchanted" lands, "shadows and noe reall Islands." Actually, according to the authority of Richard Slevin, the position of the Galápagos Archipelago, 600 miles off the western equatorial coast of South America, was roughly known to informed cartographers by the close of the sixteenth century. It appears on such early maps as those of Ortelius, 1570, Mercator, 1587, and Tatton in 1600. The Spanish, since the Pacific raids of Drake a century earlier than Davis, had not been inclined to advertise the existence of the Archipelago. It lay athwart the route of the homeward bound Pacific treasure ships.

Voyages without islands to touch upon would be epics of monotony. This was the attitude of the seventeenth century adventurers, and so it was later to prove with the time travelers in the new science of geology. We may equally expect to encounter similar views in the future annals of the astronauts. Whether for diversion of thought or for the easing of the physical body, men demand mental periods, points of reference, islands fixed in the turbulence of giant waters or, if eluding the compass, still haunting the mind like the uncertain shadows sought by Captain Davis.

William Dampier, the best of the pirate navigators, put the matter succinctly for all time when he spoke of his book of travels, *The New Voyage*, as "composed of a mixt Relation of Places and Actions in the same order of time in which they occurred." He ventured also, with a seaman's indifference to the hagglings and recriminations of scholars, that he had not bothered to compare his discoveries with those of others because, in different accounts even of the same things, some new light would be afforded by each honest observer.

Most of Dampier's life was spent with the cutlass among men of violence. He carried his journal in a section of bamboo sealed with wax against his other great antagonist, the sea. It is a miracle that he survived to reach home at all. It is perhaps an even greater miracle that a solitary buccaneer relegated to the company of rogues and scoundrels at the rim of the known world should have established a genuine claim to being the progenitor of that line of voyager naturalists which was to include Banks, Hooker, Forbes, and Darwin.

Taking the advice of the old sea rover, I shall seek in this introduction to place things and ideas in their proper relations in time and space. It will not be an easy task because the Galápagos were rightly designated the Encantadas or Enchanted Isles. As we have seen, they possessed, in older seas, an eerie quality of seeming to shift position. Yet it is from such an archipelago that the reader must begin his own *New Voyage*. The Galápagos, from the standpoint of the historian of ideas, are actually the most famous islands in the world. They belong less on the genuine equator and rather more in the latitudes of literature and science.

Dampier was the first Englishman to describe them. But, as he himself remarked, each voyager would by degrees see more and see differently. The Enchanted Isles were destined to grow more enchanted; they would play a major role in the growth of a theory in which the seeming stability of organic form was to be transmuted into something as shifting and uncertain as the shores coasted by pirates and whalermen. Even the huge land tortoises, in the language of the buccaneers, were called by such a peculiar name as Hecatee—a witch's sobriquet, the reason for whose application to turtles here at the world's end is lost, although the name was recorded by the indefatigable sailor who could not foresee the role that turtles were to play in the thought of Darwin or in the mind of that other great nineteenth-century genius and voyager, Herman Melville.

"Here," wrote Dampier, laying unknowingly a scene for the future, "the Ground is so steep, that if an Anchor starts it never holds again." The man spoke better than he knew. The solidly anchored foundations of western philosophy slipped on this ground and have never since been established with the same degree of security. A cloud was to descend upon western Christian thought—a cloud as murky as the hovering sea fogs through which Dampier and his mates on their last voyage had hunted to no avail the looming shadow of the gold-laden Manila galleon with her armament of sixty guns.

Now to Dampier and his shipmates the Galápagos, though elusive, was a place—a place from which escape was possible. Thus Lionel Wafer, one of Dampier's old associates, wrote wistfully years later of those venturesome sunny days under the Line: "We continued rambling to little purpose sometimes at sea, sometimes ashore and were then resolved to make the best of our way out of these seas." In contrast to the buccaneers, however, later comers never did find their way, at least in spirit, out of those elusive waters.

It is here that the mysterious shifting nature of this volcanic archipelago begins to assert itself. To no other oceanic isles in times known to us have come an equal number of men of the caliber of Dampier, the buccaneer navigator, Charles Darwin, voyager-naturalist, and Herman Melville, who, in the opinion of many critics, produced perhaps the greatest American novel of the nineteenth century—*Moby Dick*—a classic of the sea and of man's war with fate. No other landscape has so deflected the midnight memories of its visitors even into old age.

It is for this reason that the proper history of events must give way to "mixt Relations" and the things arising in the mind. The beasts of the Galápagos are strange and over the silence that now broods upon the islands hangs a repressed violence as of waiting events. Subterranean fires still rumble in deep caverns beneath the sea. A world is still being shaped just as the separate worlds of the three men who came there escaped their individual deaths and entered, still proliferating, into the visions of the race.

Each man saw inevitably with the eye of his time; each had his progenitors, each, in his way, also lent the unique color of his mind to what would pass beyond the observa-

tion of a few active volcanic cones projecting from the sea floor. Instead, there was destined to arise a gigantic new mythology of the shaping of the entire creation. If the word mythology unconsciously offends, then in the proper semantic usage of our time a novel scientific paradigm, evolution, may be said to be still in the process of elaboration. In that process islands, and particularly the Galápagos, were to play an early and significant role.

One may perhaps begin with Sir Francis Bacon's simple rule that one must not imagine or suppose what nature is, but rather by careful and sustained observation to determine what nature does or can be made to do. This emphasis upon the direct experience of the living world without the interference of religious or classical preconceptions is now, of course, the foundation stone of modern science. In Bacon's time, however, it was a heretical and unorthodox doctrine. Equally, the Lord Chancellor's emphasis upon experiment, that by which, as he eloquently contended, more could be achieved than in the hourglass of one man's life, made but slow progress in Elizabethan educational circles. Indeed it was only a generation after his death that the founding of the Royal Society gave evidence that Bacon's ideas had begun to permeate the minds, not so much of the schoolmen, but rather of a whole new class of enlightened and enquiring amateur scientists influenced perhaps partly by the experiences of the far-sailing voyagers.

The Spanish Main, strange natives and the mysteries of navigation were having a stimulating effect upon the minds of a previously insular people. Not alone did the reading of voyages become popular, but the rough-hewn voyagers themselves began to respond to the demand for greater accuracy and more dispassionate accounts of peoples and places visited. Dampier as an individual almost disappears from his journal, yet his simple and unaffected narration is known to have influenced the style of such literary professionals as Daniel Defoe and Jonathan Swift. The *New Voyage* formed the model for more than one fictional or satiric journey, but its importance extended beyond this: it revealed that the voyagers themselves were growing conscious of a newly forming scientific tradition. They were writing increasingly for a sophisticated public that wanted truth rather than fantasy.

Pirates and sea dogs were becoming the unacknowledged agents of the Royal Society. The truth that was wanted, however, was novel truth, truths of far lands, new faunas, peoples, and customs. It was the truths of the world that were being sought. It would not be long before the remote latitudes penetrated by the mariners would transform these geographical inquiries into an even more surprising navigational adventure—the exploration of the past. Islands would become like upthrust remnants of vanished eons emerging from the old sea floors. Even this figure of speech does not entirely express the reality. Islands are genuinely different worlds. The pasts from which they take their origin have differed at some point from the biological history of the nearest continent and therefore the plant and animal life to be found upon these bits of land is marked by differences which are enhanced by the length of time they have been isolated.:

One world, such as that of the Galápagos, may be marked by the emergence of giant turtles not to be found on neighboring coasts; another, like South Trinidad, may be dominated by land crabs; another give rise to peculiar flightless birds, of which the dodo in the Mascarene Archipelago was a perfect example. The entire continent of Australia, really a giant island long lost and disconnected from the great primary centers of evolution, constitutes, with its peculiar marsupial fauna, not a world of living fossils, but rather a world that has taken its own divergent way into the present. There is a sense, of course, in which we can say that the genetic history of every living species on the planet is unique and the solitary product of a different tempo of events. At this point, however, we would be led into unnecessary complexities. We wish only to discover in what way Christian Europe became conscious of islands as constituting a vaguely heretical threat to the orthodox view of special creation. As may be readily guessed, the observations of the voyagers played a leading role in the matter. The literature of the late eighteenth and early nineteenth centuries makes very clear the cumulative effect of the voyages of exploration.

"Trust as little as you can to report," Samuel Johnson advised a traveler, "examine all you can by your own senses." Samuel Taylor Coleridge, in his notebook of 1803, discussed the South American tree sloth and commented that since it is capable of moving only a few feet in a day when on the ground its journey from the ark on Mount Ararat must have been remarkably protracted, indicating, as Coleridge put it, "a new point in chronology."

The Baron Georges Cuvier summed up the whole contribution of the seventeenth-century Pacific voyagers through his eulogy upon the work of Sir Joseph Banks and Captain James Cook. Elaborating upon the success of their work in the Pacific, he speaks of "the creatures in some measure peculiar" with which the islands are peopled. Turning then to Australia, he observes that, if one were to except man and the dog, most of the fauna "bears no resemblance in its organic nature . . . to the rest of the world." As for the vegetables they "seem destined to subvert all our rules and systems." He ends upon a prophetic note by asserting that this "creation" is almost as new to Europe "as that of another planet." The incipient doubts as to how animals had arisen or been distributed were now beginning to be more boldly expressed than in the seventeenth century.

Since the Galápagos are our primary concern, it is of the utmost interest to mention the account of the islands given by Captain David Porter of the United States Navy. Though a professional officer engaged in commerce raiding during the war of 1812, Porter was a man of unusual observational powers who, even under the stress of war, kept an excellent record of scientific matters. His description of the huge "elephant tortoises" is invaluable historically because he saw them before the whaling ships had driven them near to extinction. It is quite apparent that Melville drew heavily for facts upon Porter's journal when composing the Encantadas.

Almost a quarter of a century before Darwin's visit Porter had recognized that the tortoises of James, Hood, and Charles islands were dissimilar and might be specifically distinct. Moreover, he had noted and described the indigenous marine iguanas which were later to attract Darwin's attention. The rocks of a cove were "covered with them and from their taking to the water very readily we were induced to believe them a distinct species from those found in the West Indies."

Porter also commented upon the lack of fear among the island birds, something which was later to attract Darwin's attention. "Doves," he writes, "of a small size, and very beautiful plumage were very numerous." There follows, however, an observation which wrings the heart of the conservationist. In miniature it is a revelation of the ways of civilized man throughout the centuries. The doves, he continues, "afforded great amusement to the younger part of the crew in killing them with sticks and stones, which was in no way difficult as they were very tame." In a similar fashion the iguanas, first feared, were discovered to be timid. Immediately hundreds were killed with clubs. This wanton, savage slaughter seems to have left Porter undisturbed. It was typical of a man-centered viewpoint which throughout the nineteenth century devastated the natural resources of North America.

Most surprising, however, is Captain Porter's geological sophistication. He was scientifically alert enough to know that the islands were of volcanic origin probably at no distant period. Of this he was convinced by the innumerable craters and freshly exposed beds of lava. In contrast to Captain Fitzroy of the Beagle, whose undeviating fundamentalism was something of a burden to his shipmate Charles Darwin, Porter, a generation earlier, proposed a conundrum while affecting indifference. "I shall leave others," he says, "to account for the manner in which all those islands obtained their supply of tortoises and guanas [iguanas], and other animals of the reptile kind; it is not my business even to conjecture as to the cause. I shall merely state, that those islands have every appearance of being newly created, and that those perhaps are the only part of the animal creation that could subsist on them . . . Nature has created them elsewhere and why could she not do it as well on those islands?"

In spite of Porter's emphasis on facts and his discreet refusal to speculate, there is here clearly presented in the journal of a man of action the growing doubts already harbored by scholars about the likelihood of the world having been populated from a single primary geographical center, as had been so long assumed. Moreover, Porter had stated with marked directness that the islands were geologically young. This could only imply that some undiminished creative force was still abroad on the planet—a force best glimpsed at work upon lonely island shores. To derive the faunas of islands from a solitary center or even single time of creation, said an anonymous reviewer of 1831, "scarcely falls within the sphere of credibility."

Before Darwin set sail upon his immortal voyage the term "centers of creation" was beginning to supplant "creation" in the vocabulary of biologists. They may not, all of them, have foreseen where this semantic shift was to lead but, in retrospect, it may be observed that vague though the phrase now sounds, it was leading deliberately and surely to the recognition of organic change, in other words to the discovery of evolution.

Intense effort went into the study of the dispersal of life. As a consequence, one begins to encounter references to species like the dodo "newly called into being" because they had never been encountered outside the islands of their discovery. Today the phrase "center of creation," which occurs in the account of the voyage of the *Beagle*, has sometimes been ascribed to Darwin's coinage as a clever euphemism for evolution. In actuality, the doctrine of separate specific centers for the emergence of species was of sustained biological importance throughout the first half of the nineteenth century. It vanished only when it was supplanted by the full recognition of evolution after the publication of the *Origin of Species*. The pre-Darwinian botanist D. C. Wildenow's penetrating observation that "what appears to be nothing but desolation and death, is the theatre of a new world in miniature," was destined to receive late but dramatic confirmation in the Galápagos.

II. CHARLES DARWIN

"Between the La Plata and the Rio Colorado," so the old records of the eighteen-thirties run, "is a low half-drowned coast, extremely dangerous. With the examination of these dangers began the work of the survey."

The half-drowned coastline is that of eastern South America. Its explorers in the early nineteenth century were Captain King of the *Adventure*, and Robert Fitzroy who commanded, upon the associated voyage, her majesty's ship *Beagle*, a vessel which was to have a peculiar significance to the modern world of science. Charles Darwin had sailed as a young man in the *Beagle* as naturalist under Fitzroy's command. Their names were to be indissolubly associated because, upon that voyage, Charles Darwin became convinced of the reality of evolution. Indeed the cartographic instructions given to Captain Fitzroy by the British Hydrographical Office are oddly prophetic: "Of this kind of half-knowledge we have had too much; the present state of science, which affords such ample means, seems to demand that whatever is now done should be finally done; and that coasts which are constantly visited by English vessels should no longer have the motley appearance of alternate error and accuracy."

Like Fitzroy the scientific navigator, Charles Darwin was to pass beyond his forerunners who had caught similarly disturbing, if sporadic glimpses, into a remote country of phantasmal change—the domain of our evolutionary past. Darwin, with the publication of the *Origin of Species*, a quarter of a century after his adventure upon a "half-drowned coast," would reveal a navigator's chart of the unsounded depths of time that would point the way to the triumphs of modern biology and succeed in reinterpreting man's whole conception of life. The beginnings of great scientific achievements are often small, and hidden in a past more remote than that encompassed in the triangulations of the Admiralty's cartographers. As avid readers of biography we are apt to see our admired geniuses in solitary perspective, as they appear on a great voyage. We conceive them as deriving their inspiration from heaven in a lightning flash and owing little or nothing to their predecessors. The truth is frequently more commonplace though just as fascinating.

Darwin, the youthful naturalist, peering through the smother of surf upon a chartless shore, was figuratively seeing farther than his shipmates knew. He was enabled to do so, not solely out of innate genius, but because others also had seen distantly, if not much, and had set down their speculations. The youth on the *Beagle* had, by descent, training, and inclination, been exposed since childhood to broad educational vistas in a period of rapid intellectual change.

He was born in the precise year, 1809, that the Frenchman, Jean Baptiste Lamarck, published his *Philosophie Zoologique* in which a theory of evolution was propounded —based largely on the assumed inherited effects of habit. England, caught in the throes of conservative reaction against the French revolution and its aftermath, would dismiss the idea out of hand. Lamarck's tentative but sometimes acute insights would never receive wholehearted attention in England in either his or Darwin's lifetime. Nevertheless one of Darwin's future teachers at Edinburgh, Robert Grant, had read Lamarck and had become, as a consequence, a rejected pioneer advocate in Britain of the evolutionary hypothesis.

Charles Darwin was born in a family of physicians. His grandfather Erasmus had jousted intellectually with Samuel Johnson, associated with scholars in the Lunar Society, and written poetry which, popular for a time, fell precipitously out of fashion. The verse, it may be noted, advocated evolutionary views and was elaborately footnoted with many keen observations upon natural history. Erasmus was a lusty eighteenth-century character rather frowned upon by the later generation of Victorian Darwins. His son Robert, Charles Darwin's father, had never expressed much affection for Erasmus, and although Charles, in his later years, prepared a small biography of his grandfather, it is painfully pedestrian and does not satisfactorily analyze Erasmus' gifts as a naturalist.

It has been noted by more than one observer that father-son relationships were somewhat strained throughout the three generations, culminating in Charles' emergence as a major scientist. Mingled with strong-willed family temperament was the additional stress produced by early nineteenth-century conservatism following upon a more tolerant and enquiring age. Victorian paternal dominance was absolute and, in the case of Charles, the early death of his mother removed any softening feminine influence upon the relations between Charles and his domineering father. Although Charles was eight years old when his mother died, he was to write many years after with labored reserve: "It is odd that I can remember hardly anything about her except her death bed."

Charles Darwin was regarded as a very ordinary if not backward child by his father who, nevertheless, intended to make a physician of him. The family had plentiful means through both the maternal and paternal lines. Charles' early schooling had largely been conducted at home in Shrewsbury. Later he attended a private school in the town and after acquiring a smattering of the classics and a taste for Gilbert White's *Natural History of Selborne* he was packed off at sixteen by his father's edict to the University of Edinburgh to become a physician.

One must be a little wary of Darwin's reminiscences upon educational matters. He hated and despised the classical education of his time. It is also evident that this distaste extended to the medical world. "Awful," "dull," are included in some of his comments upon lectures. Some of the men referred to are regarded as among the great medical teachers of the age. We may thus suspect that the teen-age Darwin was not always objective in his judgments. He fled from the unavoidable cruelties of operations performed without anaesthetics, and it grew ever more evident that the medical profession offered no attractions. His time, instead, was spent visiting naturalists and in collecting.

Dr. Grant, the Lamarckian evolutionist to whom we have previously alluded, undoubtedly had an influence upon Charles. Later a coolness developed between the older man and his pupil so that they dropped out of each others lives. It should not be forgotten, however, that Grant was one of the few avowed evolutionists in the early part of the century. His hand can be suspected in at least one anonymous paper in an Edinburgh magazine. It is evident that he was never a believer in the catastrophic geology of his time. He wrote, for example, in 1838: "The unity of the plan of organization, and the regular succession of animal forms, point out a beginning of this great kingdom on the surface of our globe, although the earliest stages may now be effaced; and the continuity of the series through all geological epochs, and the gradual transitions which connect the species of one formation with those of the next in succession, distinctly indicate that they form parts of one creation . . ."

Robert Jameson, another of young Charles' instructors who was later to be excoriated as "an old brown dry stick," is treated with more kindness by James Ritchie, who later held the same chair at Edinburgh. "Darwin," he says, "picked up his early knowledge of nature in Jameson's classroom and on the shores of the Firth of Forth." Darwin was peculiarly inimical to formal instruction. In later years he failed to recognize that the universities whose curricula he scorned had, nevertheless, assembled the men who opened for him, informally though it may have been, the doorway leading to his career.

Two years sufficed at Edinburgh. His disgusted father,

hurling at Charles the epithet "rat catcher," hustled him off to Cambridge and the career of a clergyman. He spent three years at the University where again he was at loose ends in spite of his dutiful attempt to read for Holy Orders. As at Edinburgh, he associated mainly with naturalists. His most fortunate contact lay in his friendship with the sensitive and gentle botanist John Henslow. In the end it was Henslow's good offices that secured for Darwin his post under Robert Fitzroy as naturalist on the voyage of the *Beagle*, which sailed for its five-year cruise around the world in December of 1831. Only under the urging of Josiah Wedgwood, Charles' uncle, had Robert Darwin given a reluctant consent to this mad enterprise.

The *Beagle* was a lumbering, ill-sailing brig burst over by winter storms. Darwin, down with seasickness, huddled in his bunk and thought of home. About and over him in the sea-darkness passed hoarse cries and commands. A long life's journey had begun, but it had started, not under the swinging sea lamps in 1831, but reading in youth grandfather's *Zoonomia* and talking earnestly with Robert Grant in Edinburgh. Those significant days would in the end be ill-recorded, but he had brought them, hidden in his mind, upon the long voyage of the *Beagle*. Here they would gestate in the solitary nights at sea or when he rode alone upon Andean uplands. In 1835 he wrote to his friend Henslow:

"I cannot tell you how I enjoyed some of these views—it is worth coming from England once to feel such intense delight; at an elevation from 10,000 to 12,000 feet there is a transparency in the air, and a confusion of distances and a sort of stillness which gives the sensation of being in another world, and when to this is joined the picture so plainly drawn of great epochs of violence, it causes in the mind a most strange assemblage of ideas."

Strange and motley his meditations must have been. Darwin in later years was to assert that "save for a few vague doubts" his thoughts were perfectly orthodox while upon his travels. Nevertheless Captain Fitzroy is known to have protested that he had often chided Darwin upon heretical views expressed during the voyage.

In fact, one year prior to the letter written above, we have another intriguing document confided to the patient and tolerant Henslow. There is the same intoxication with high air and sunlight natural to a fog-bound Britisher. In it Charles speaks of plains "abounding with organic remains which perhaps I may have the good luck to catch in the very act of moving . . ." By "moving," it would appear Darwin meant changing, altering—the discovery of extinct life caught anatomically in the act of flowing onward. It seems evident that in old age Darwin confused his

own later discovery of natural selection as the mechanism of evolution with his earlier youthful suspicion that evolution had taken place. In actuality there is some documentary reason to suspect that he was a Lamarckist at heart throughout the voyage, but a dissatisfied one who continued to brood over the inadequacies of the Lamarckian explanation of organic change.

Whatever ideas Darwin may have entertained at this time, however, his thoughts were undergoing a considerable revision. He was reading in South America the first edition of Sir Charles Lyell's *Principles of Geology*—a book which was destined to overthrow the Christian conception of time as surely as Charles Darwin was later to alter our whole conception of the development of life, man included. Lyell, like Darwin, had his pioneer forerunners, but he was a great and solid generalist, trained originally for the law, careful with his evidence and possessing a judicious and balanced style. He was never prolix, never hortatory, cautious but not dogmatic. He was, in fact, one of the founders of modern geology, and before his reasoning there capitulated a miscellaneous and archaic assemblage of Biblical geologists and catastrophists who had tried to read from the rock strata evidences of successive world-wide upheavals and extinctions with renewed supernatural creation of more advanced forms of life. In the strictest terms Lyell laid down the modern foundations of geology:

"We hear of sudden violent revolutions.
I shall adopt a different course.
We are not authorized in the infancy of our Science to recur to extraordinary agents."

With these words and his assembled evidence Lyell dismissed the supernatural fumes and vapors that had hovered like a visible miasma over the geological past. Time now unrolled before the geologist's eye almost infinite in extent. The forces at work upon the planet were no longer incomprehensible and ghostly. They consisted of frost and running water, the age-long fall of leaves and wind-borne dust. Through millions of unrecorded years these, and forces like them, had been the unseen shapers of the planet's surface. No man had properly assessed the potential for change that lurked in a puff of wind or the fall of a raindrop. One had to multiply these tiny events by millions of years to arrive at the destruction of a mountain range.

In the moment of reading the *Principles of Geology*, young Darwin began to model himself upon Charles Lyell. "I am become a jealous disciple," he wrote to a cousin, the Reverend Fox. "I am tempted to carry parts to a greater extent even than he does." Darwin at this point began to wonder whether additional effort spent upon animals "would not have been of more certain value." Prophetically, in the same letter, he spoke with eagerness of the Galápagos Islands, the next stop in the wandering itinerary of the *Beagle*. There was just one way in which Darwin might pass beyond Charles Lyell. The latter had established the infinite time needed by the evolutionist for the invisible pace of organic evolution. In spite of this effort, and in spite of much perceptive probing into biological matters, Lyell had publicly dismissed Lamarck. While recognizing that extinction took place, Lyell had failed to propose any form of replacement in the shape of evolutionary change. He had recognized time but had not explained the novelties introduced within it by the transformations of the living substance.

Lyell had performed the stupendous feat of getting short-lived man to recognize and examine the natural but hidden powers that transformed the landscape. Before life, however, Lyell stood abashed. It seemingly defied all efforts at rational explanation and it was to rational principles that Lyell was devoted. For the moment, he thought, it was better to accept life's seeming stability. The general public was shaken enough by the discovery of the antiquity of the globe. People were not yet emotionally prepared to examine the dark stairwell of the past out of which mankind had so painfully clambered.

The sea voyage since antiquity has been an enlightener of the human mind. By the eighteenth century, and after the first great circumnavigations, a paradox did not escape the sea rovers: that the winds which bore them westward into the future, into new and unmapped realms, finally brought them round into the ancient East. Eventually they dropped their anchors, these forward-looking captains, in the sleepy harbors of the farther past. It was on such an unexpected occasion in 1835 that the *Beagle* rang down her anchor in a cove at Chatham Island in the Galápagos. "The natural history of this archipelago," Darwin was later to comment, "is very remarkable: it seems to be a little world in itself; the greater number of its inhabitants, both vegetable and animal, being found nowhere else."

Stark basaltic lavas lay baking under the noonday sun. Great black lizards four feet long drowsed on the coastal rocks. In the interior of the islands were well-beaten paths worn by the dragging bodies of hundreds of giant tortoises. Nowhere else in the modern world, Darwin was afterward to muse, "did the reptilian order replace the herbivorous mammalia in so extraordinary a manner." If Darwin had not arrived at the farther past he had indeed stumbled upon a surprising replica. The leafless shrubs and the huge reptiles suggested an antediluvian world that had, in some manner, drowsed its way into the present.

Moreover, Darwin had stumbled upon a secret that seemed to call in question even the conception that "centers of creation" produced entirely similar species of animals. In what was apparently a perfectly uniform tropic environment the young naturalist found, as had Porter before him, that the turtles of the different islands were distinguishable, that the finches, a common enough bird on the nearby continent, here possessed an astonishing variety of modifications, particularly in their beaks. This circumstance, he felt, suggested different habits upon different islands. No other part of the five-year voyage of the *Beagle* was to make such an impression upon Darwin. He bewailed the fate that hurried him away from the archipelago. Years after he would write to Moritz Wagner that "it was such cases as that of the Galápagos . . . which chiefly led me to study the origin of species."

Truly the Encantadas, the Enchanted Isles, were what the name implied. Here was a world in miniature, an isolated world six hundred miles from the South American coast. But on a score or more of similar islets incipient differences existed among the plants and animals. They differed from their continental relatives and they differed on their individual islands—volcanic upthrust hummocks that were young by the world's time. The concept of specific centers of creation was an illusion unless each creature was itself a center. Nor was this the life of the Biblical creation. It was younger. Also it was strangely altered. Did life then retain some invisible creative power within itself that had nothing to do with existence in a superficially similar environment or climate? Was some terrible, slow-moving but inexorable force remaking even man beneath the seemingly substantial body in which he dwelt? Rightly seen by the eye of genius, the Galápagos were a rift, a chink, a keyhole into time. Darwin jotted hastily in his notebook as the *Beagle* hoisted sail.

The rest of Darwin's global voyage would be anticlimactic. Something of the weariness of wandering Odysseus enters his letters. From St. Helena he wrote to Henslow: "Oh the degree to which I long to be once again living quietly with not one single novel object near me!" To his sister Susan he protested, "I loathe, I abhor the sea." Once his shame over his failures at school and his timidity before his father arose to haunt him. Toward the end of the voyage he wrote to his friend Fox: "I dare hardly look forward to the future, for I do not know what will become of me."

For the moment he had exhausted his own resources. "The greatest natural genius," wisely observed the noted painter Sir Joshua Reynolds, "cannot subsist on its own stock; he who resolves never to ransack any mind but his own will soon be reduced from mere barrenness to the poorest of all imitations. It is vain to invent without materials on which the mind may work, and from which invention must originate. Nothing can come of nothing."*

Buffon had once contended that genius is a long patience. Darwin had proved his patience, but unaided observation, even with the help of Lyell, was not enough. Now would come the careful probing into the work of other men, the effort toward a new and startling synthesis.

Darwin, as we have seen, had not been unimpressed by his South American experience before reaching the Galápagos. Until he set foot upon the Islands, however, his tentative thoughts upon evolution had been involved with wide continental sweeps of country or, as in his search for fossils on the pampas, with deep plunges into the past. The Galápagos presented quite a different problem which can best be presented by the later comment of Darwin's friend, the botanist Sir Joseph Hooker, who refers to the island faunal and floral differences as *"a most strange fact, and one which quite overturns all our preconceived notions of species radiating from a centre."* From an emphasis upon exterior climatic factors or "creative power" in a given area, the individuality manifested among the species in the many islets left quite another impression: that the force involved in organic change, if change indeed existed, must be focused in the individual organism, not in the world outside. The Galápagos were geologically similar in structure and in climate. They were, in truth, a tiny world of islets separated only by shifting sea currents. Not alone did they contain creatures strangely altered from those of the nearest continent, but the forms isolated on the individual islands separated only by short stretches of sea seemed also to be continuing to diverge as though there were a hidden magic in isolation itself.

This concealed magic was not immediately grasped by Darwin. In fact, some remarks of the Vice Governor of the islands, a man whose name survives only as Mr. Lawson, first called Darwin's attention to the diversity among the island turtles shortly before his departure. It was this conversation which had occasioned Darwin's outburst of regret upon being swept away from the Galápagos upon an unreturning wind. Nevertheless, a fertile seed had been planted in Darwin's mind, though as yet he could offer no rational explanation for what had been observed. Almost a quarter of a century would pass before his epoch-making book the *Origin of Species* would be offered to the world.

Darwin settled quietly into smoky London in 1836.

The island problem continued to haunt him. It was evident that he regarded it as an important clue to the nature of the evolutionary mechanism. Nevertheless while his great hunt went on he built a sober reputation for himself in the more mundane fields of science. His father had apparently become reconciled to his pursuits and the family wealth insured the security of the diligent young man. He came to be a respected figure in scientific circles and an intimate of the same Sir Charles Lyell whose geological work had so profoundly affected him.

"I shall probably do little more," Darwin remarked lugubriously two years after seeing his account of the voyage of the *Beagle* through the press. "I shall be content to admire the strides others make in science." Though by this time the great synthesis of the *Origin of Species* existed in his mind, Darwin was baffled by ill health of a nature now generally suspected of being at least partly psychosomatic, but which in his time was frequently ascribed to the debilitating effects of seasickness or other obscure physical causes. About 1840 Darwin moved with his young wife Emma to the village of Downe some nineteen miles from London where he became, in his own words "a hermit." Here he reared his family and lived out the rest of his days in the unobtrusive pursuit of his favorite subject, natural history.

Though we know that by 1837 he possessed the key to the great secret which had eluded him in the Galapagos, a strong reluctance to publish kept his pen immobilized. Over twenty years were to elapse before a chance anticipation by Alfred Russel Wallace, a wandering biological collector, was to force his hand. The odd way in which the *Origin* was produced and the story of its twenty-two year gestation has both fortunate and unfortunate aspects. The delay resulted in an enormous accumulation of evidence, far more than was ever published, but it also reveals something of Darwin's anxieties, if not compulsions, and his reluctance to engage in public controversy. Furthermore it increases the difficulty of tracing the genesis of his ideas.

At one time, and this is subconsciously revelatory, Darwin even made a will in which he set aside a sum of money to allow a choice from among several possible scholars whom he respected, to complete the work. The act appears to suggest an unconscious death wish, a desire to transfer a publicly unpleasant task to a scapegoat. At the same time, the attraction of the subject was such that the volume could not be abandoned or totally transferred to others. One could work upon it endlessly but procrasti-

*Cited in W. J. Bates, *Criticism: the Modern Texts*, N.Y. 1952

nate. In no other book was he so dilatory, yet secretly it was his passion, and he labored upon it, as he himself tells us, when he could do nothing else from illness.

"The earth," once remarked Antoine de Saint Exupéry, "gives man more self-knowledge than all the books, because it offers resistance to him and it is only in conflict with forces outside himself that man finds the way to himself." Perhaps it is for this reason that Charles Darwin and Alfred Russel Wallace were the first scientists completely to visualize the significance of natural selection, for both were wanderers in the earth's wild places. Nevertheless they had their more timid anticipators. These were strollers along hedgerows in the English lanes at home— men pursuing the tradition of Gilbert White of Selborne. One of these men, Edward Blyth of Ealing, poor, and afflicted with ill health, now appears to have been one of Darwin's primary, if unacknowledged, catalysts in the discovery of natural selection. For over a hundred years his work has been lost in obscurity.

The orthodox interpretation of the discovery of natural selection which has been current for over a hundred years and is still actively defended, particularly in Britain, runs somewhat as follows: that Darwin "working upon true Baconian principles," as he once expressed it, "and without any theory collected facts on a wholesale scale." Leaving aside the question of whether any scholar would be impelled to collect facts wholesale without at least the glimmerings of an idea to guide him, we may proceed to the second part of the legend; namely, that Darwin read Thomas Malthus' book on population in October of 1838 and was so struck with the human facts there presented upon the geometric growth of populations versus the purely arithmetical increase in the food supply that the principle of natural selection leaped immediately into his mind. Without wishing to denigrate the importance of Malthus in nineteenth-century thinking, we can confidently assert that the story of natural selection is more complicated than this version of events would suggest.

Natural selection is a phrase introduced by Darwin to denote what is, in essence, a selective death rate which promotes the survival of those creatures whose genetic qualities most successfully meet the needs of a given environment. The struggle for existence, in other words, is the winnowing mechanism which determines survival in a biologically variable population. Given the great span of geological time, and the constant tendency of living forms to produce mutations, selection should result in the slow and insensible alteration of living forms. More than struggle is involved, however. Isolation such as that found upon the individual islands of the Galapagos may preserve species which would be destroyed under continental conditions. Indeed it may open doorways for divergent evolution into unoccupied environmental niches of the sort penetrated by Darwin's curious assemblage of diversified finches. These factors we might designate together as the change-promoting or liberalizing aspect of natural selection as propounded by Charles Darwin in the *Origin of Species.*

The layman frequently does not realize that natural selection has another, a conservative or form-stabilizing aspect, which is also perfectly valid. Its significance in the Darwinian story was submerged and well-nigh lost for the simple reason that Darwin not alone attached a new name to an old concept but, in addition, drastically revised its import. Thus the idea took on what seemed to be a most startling novelty.

No discoverer, however, is without forerunners least of all a scientist. The concept of natural selection, like the animals the evolutionist studies, has an evolving history. The idea, but not in its creative aspect of indefinite organic change, was known prior to the nineteenth century. It existed, however, under other names. To observe this is not to detract one iota from the insight of Charles Darwin or the superlative character of his achievement. The historical key to our problem lies rather in the intellectual climate of the eighteenth and early nineteenth centuries. Sometimes when our model of the world changes, an old idea is not abandoned. It is merely discovered to have hitherto unguessed potentialities which are not always immediately glimpsed.

The eighteenth century lay under the spell of Newton and the conception of a carefully balanced world machine. This machine, divinely ordained and kept from deviating error by a God who began insensibly to take on the attributes of a watchmaker, held life, as well as astronomical affairs, in a self-stabilizing balance. There was a struggle for existence, later to compose part of the Darwinian creed, but the pendulum was always assumed to swing back to "normal," to the familiar appearance of the existing world. So long as the short Christian time-scale of six thousand years was literally accepted, there could be no time for evolution to take place. The struggle for existence that resulted in selection was constantly referred to in the pre-Darwinian literature as "natural government," "pruning," or "policing." Thus life was kept in its proper balance and "fit" for its ordained environment. Everything was held in its proper ecological sphere and maintained there. The deviant, the white stag, the albino blackbird, was struck down. As late as 1857 in the *Quarterly Journal of the Geological Society of London* we find the president of the Society remarking that "the carnivora in each period of the world's history [fulfil] their destined office—to check excess in the progress of life and maintain the balance of creation."

Two events, however, began to cast a growing shadow over this neatly ordered picture of the world. The eighteenth century scholar James Hutton of Edinburgh, and Lyell, later on in Darwin's youth, introduced to the world of science the specter of illimitable time—time in which, it became increasingly evident, life could not always have borne the shapes it does today. Thus the eternal balance fell into question—though various makeshift compromises with theology persisted for some decades.

Second, and more obscurely, the growing demands of the new industrial towns created an increased need for wool, meat, milk, and vegetables. Artificial selection among domestic animals and plants came into vogue. The rule-of-thumb breeder, the careful gardener, began to discover that individual animals and plants varied amazingly and that many of these variations were heritable. Horses, dogs, cattle, and poultry in skilled hands could be altered in a few generations. As yet nobody saw where this was leading; no one could make out a connection between this humanly directed process and the seemingly fixed species boundaries ordained by nature. What intelligent force could possibly select and control the genetic traits of plants and animals in an unattended wilderness?

Thus the matter stood, but a latent dynamism was being sensed in nature, *potential change* that only the eighteenth-century world machine could hold to an undeviating balance. One can sense in the literature a growing impression that change is biologically *possible* but actually never realizable in a balanced Newtonian universe. Lyell phrased his version of natural selection as a "principle of preoccupancy." New, aberrant forms could never by competition secure a foothold upon territory held by fully adapted prior inhabitants.

In 1835 the young naturalist Edward Blyth devised what he called a "localising principle" in which he went further than Lyell into the genetics of the subject. He described, in fact, what we would now call "natural selection." At first he portrayed its conservative aspect only—the close adaptation of the animal to its existing environment. Today the modern biologist would have to admit that natural selection has actually two separate and partially opposed faces. One aspect is the comparatively short-time selection which preserves the appearance of a given species and lends apparent stability to the living world about us. In this process lurks the conservative, form-preserving aspect of nature that maintains rather than

alters the existing web of life. This is the "natural government," the balanced order which delighted most of the thinkers of the eighteenth century. It is the face of the natural world as that world has always been seen by short-lived man.

Paradoxically, there is another hidden aspect of this world, as Darwin was to prove. This same "natural government" under his new term "natural selection" allowed for an unexpected emergent novelty extending into the remote past. Time and genetic variability moved behind the visible face of things like the hour hand of a clock. Man simply did not contain geological memory. He had not rightly read the story of change that was indelibly impressed in his own body. He did not understand the immensity of the time scale in which short term "balance" gives way to insensible long term change.

Natural selection incorporates two equally valid propositions, but one had been understood well over fifty years before the other. In short, every living thing possesses both seeming changelessness and a shape-shifting invisible reality hidden in the cells of the body. Both the lumbering turtles and the delicate finches of the Galápagos had equally possessed that fairy quality. Without being sure, this was what Darwin had briefly and tentatively sensed in the final hours before the *Beagle* weighed anchor. The mystery which had enticed him would not for one moment be forgotten. It would haunt him through the streets of London.

Edward Blyth, in the *Magazine of Natural History*, a biological journal which we know was sent to Darwin even while on the voyage of the *Beagle*, had described and recognized the factor that to our casual eye restricts variation within bounds. He made the observation, frequently first ascribed to Darwin, that there is a true relationship between artificial and natural selection. He argued that the best adapted creature will leave more offspring and thus transmit to oncoming generations its improved qualities. Blyth contended, however, like others before him, that selection will thus maintain or enhance in a wild state the best *present* qualities of the species. Thus Blyth recognized the genetic trend toward deviation, but he first assumes that only man, through isolation and artificial selection, can promote the rise of new varieties. Time and geological change are not yet seen to offer the same controls briefly exercised by the breeder. Two years later, however, in that momentous year of 1837 when young Charles Darwin opened the first notebook that was to lead to the *Origin of Species*, young Blyth, in the *Magazine of Natural History*, wrote the following:

"A variety of important considerations here crowd upon

the mind, foremost of which is the enquiry that, as man, by removing species from their appropriate haunts super-induces changes on their physical constitution and adaptations, to what extent may not the same take place in wild nature, so that, in a few generations, distinctive characters may be acquired, such as are recognized as indicative of specific diversity. *May not then, a large proportion of what are considered species have descended from a common heritage?*" [Italics mine. L.E.]

Edward Blyth had ventured by a series of stepping stones into a magic realm from which, after an awe-inspiring vision, he had timidly retreated. Darwin, immersed in a gigantic reading program of years, studied Blyth's papers. We know this from Darwin's notes preserved in the Cambridge Library, though he was never to allude to them in print. Their influence upon him is apparent in ways too indelible to erase. He was prepared, as Blyth was not, to enter the new world of change. He had visited the Enchanted Isles.

Darwin once confessed to the historian John Morley that he was "deficient in the historical sense." He is also known to have once expressed the opinion that he who succeeds in impressing upon the public a new point of view deserves essentially all the credit that may accrue to him. There are defenders of Darwin's attitude who would say Darwin dealt in fact, not speculation, and owed nothing to theorizers. Certainly he accumulated perhaps the greatest and most diverse body of fact ever amassed in the demonstration of a single hypothesis. Yet consider the persistent ambiguity within the man. He was capable of writing to his close friend Joseph Hooker: "I look at a strong tendency to generalise as an entire evil," while discoursing to Alfred Russel Wallace: "I am a firm believer that without speculation there is no good and original observation." Indeed it was "speculative men" whom he wanted to read his book.

Whatever the motives that caused the long, compulsive labor upon natural selection which Alfred Russel Wallace cut short in 1858 by the independent enunciation, in a letter to Darwin, of the same hypothesis, one may be thankful for their existence. Wallace had forced Darwin out of his hermitage, but when the great book which Darwin regarded as a mere summary of his labors hastily appeared, the time was ripe for it. Moreover, the massive weight of the twenty years' accumulation of evidence would never be lightly overthrown. Charles Darwin had taken the sane, conservative, "natural" government of the eighteenth century and shown it to be an illusion. Instead, the whole of life was, in Wallace's words, "subject to indefinite departure."

Darwin was gentle. There is reason to believe that he was kind to Edward Blyth when the latter came back to England after years of ill health in India. Whatever was known between them, or forgotten, we will probably never know. There is a curious ironic twist, however, in a remark Charles made to Joseph Hooker when the *Origin* was well on the way to assured fame. "It is an old subject of grief to me," remarked the great naturalist, "that the very best men read so little, and give up nearly their whole time to original work. I have often thought that Science would progress more if there was more reading."

Darwin had had the best of both worlds—the wilderness and the library. Among the great biologists of the nineteenth century—the last of the great amateurs—he was destined to be singularly fortunate. Lamarck had died in poverty under the humiliating ridicule of his contemporaries. The discoveries of Gregor Mendel, the founder of modern genetics, were not even recognized by nineteenth-century science and his death went unattended. Darwin, like William Dampier, after wanderings in which disease or accident might readily have struck him down, reached at last the safety of his refuge at Downe.

Even in his fame, platform appearances proved unnecessary. His battles were so well fought for him by his aggressive and articulate co-worker, Thomas Huxley, that in the year of Darwin's death in 1882, an American biologist, Theodore Gill, was able to speak of the *Origin* in words still true today:

"It would indeed, have been a bold man who would have predicted that, in two decades after its appearance, the views therein promulgated would be universally accepted and be taken as the recognized platform of biologists. But the incredible has actually happened . . ."

This is not to say that today's biologists see eye to eye with Darwin on all points. He labored in a field of ever widening peripheries. Like all scientific discoverers he is a transitional figure retaining something of the past while peering into the future.

Darwin was essentially a field naturalist in the old tradition. It has been remarked by Merle Bevington that the *Origin* was almost the last great scientific book that a person without scientific training could feel competent to read and judge. As for Darwin, he was willing to say of his life work: "I look at it as absolutely certain that very much in the *Origin* will be proved rubbish; but I expect and hope that the framework will stand." After the passage of a hundred years the words ring true. The framework has been enriched and embellished, but it stands.

A particulate, purely descriptive science involving the individual oddities of wolves and pigeons, woodpeckers and tortoises—isolated objects in an inexplicable universe—had been suddenly caught up and made rational in a vast, comprehensive synthesis. The variations written into the particles of life had proved in their way as invisibly potent harbingers of change as the scampering imprints of the raindrops whose significance Lyell had detected long ago upon a fossil beach. The one man, Lyell, had projected far into forgotten eons the silent forces of the existing world and shown the enormity of their power to effect geologic change. The other, Darwin, in the recognition of minute variation acted upon by selection, had grasped the emergent novelty contained in the germs of life. All that is today different and fragmented, was once one; all that now is, contains the unimaginable and still diverging future. Charles Darwin had given man the power to understand his relationship to the entire living creation, and in that understanding to transcend his origins or be destroyed by them.

III. HERMAN MELVILLE

Just as the principle of natural selection was finally observed to contain two paradoxical and somewhat opposed propositions, so Herman Melville, the novelist, may be said to present a complementary facet to the thought of Darwin. The latter was concerned solely with the creative aspects of the struggle for existence—the struggle itself he took for granted. Melville's name is not recorded in the annals of science but he saw, nevertheless, in the uncanny machine of nature, one enchanted ingredient that Darwin failed to report: "All things that most exasperate and outrage mortal man," wrote the author of *Moby Dick*, "all these things are bodiless, but only bodiless as subjects not as agents." It is a bodiless abstraction, perhaps life itself, that Melville detected in the dumb and ponderous persistence of the monster turtles of the Galápagos. These are the agents which he found crawling beneath the foundations of the world, as if they were both the victims and the armored receptacles of an extraordinary power.

Few writers early in their career have unconsciously revealed such a poignant forewarning of the nature of their interior landscape as did Herman Melville. *Typee* and *Omoo*, his two earliest and most successful books, are essentially picaresque accounts of the adventures of young Melville while serving before the mast and jumping ship, as did so many sailors, among the Eden-like islands of the central Pacific. These books, read in his time far more widely than his grim sea-classic, *Moby Dick*, exercised a profound influence upon the South Sea literature which thereafter arose and persisted down into the twentieth century.

Much of this literature was idyllic and escapist. Melville, however, in the early chapters of *Omoo* describes his encounter with a white renegade named Lem Hardy, who through the possession of a musket and a bag of ammunition had become the petty tyrant of a little island kingdom. Across Hardy's forehead, viewed with misgivings by the astonished seamen, was indelibly tattooed in blue the figure of a monstrous shark. Can it be, one wonders in retrospect, if something of that dread creature lingered symbolically in Melville's mind, slowly, by some native magic, transforming itself into the vast overwhelming leviathan Moby Dick—the fateful master of all seas? Or is it not equally possible that in the fortuitous glimpse of that inked shape imprinted upon a stranger's brow something surfaced that had been lurking concealed in the illimitable seas of Melville's thought?

Omoo constitutes the last product of Melville's youth. From then on the easy civilities of society became for him more difficult to endure. He brooded upon and despised his earlier successes. The incessant voyager had turned inward to the mind's restless seas and was already afloat with Ahab beating frantically to sea off a lee shore. The great hunt symbolized in *Moby Dick* had already begun.

At this point we may well pause to consider what contrasts, analogies or relationships exist between the sober scientific pursuits of Charles Darwin and a novelist who had reason to fear he would be remembered only as a man who had lived among cannibals.

To begin with the obvious, Charles Darwin and Herman Melville were contemporaries, save that Melville was ten years younger, having been born in 1819. It was some six years after the visit of the *Beagle* that the young American, as a foremast hand, had set eyes upon the scoriae and monstrous tortoises of the Galápagos. By the time he wrote the *Encantadas*, as an episodic serial for Putnam's magazine in 1854, he was so far out of favor as a writer that he used a pseudonym.

Many critics have either ignored the work or given it but slight attention. The separate pieces, though originally intended as a connected whole, have seemed to lack continuity save for a common purgatorial landscape. Nothing so dramatic as the great White Whale appears to cross our vision. The fleeting human characters appear largely as "isolatos," victims of circumstance or extravagances of character almost as exuberant and distorted as some of the island fauna itself. There is no Ahab here to challenge fate and go down with his doomed vessel into the deep maw of the sea. Here in the Galápagos is to be found only a Caliban-like bestiality or, in the case of the Chola widow, a noble, sustained endurance in the fires of an earthly inferno. Whatever is taking place represents another aspect of Melville's mind than the whale hunt, something undramatized by corpusants or harpoons forged in blood.

The movement, if there can be said to be movement in these narratives, leaves an odd impression of suspended time, or rather of time immeasurable—geologic time. To these islands, in Melville's words, "change never comes, neither the change of seasons nor of sorrows." Darwin, as a biologist, sensed with quickening curiosity the hint of slow organic alteration. Melville, however, was not wrong in his own impression that over the islands brooded some agelong disastrous spell which had confined the chief sound of life among its cactus thickets and ravines to a reptilian hiss.

There is something about Melville's treatment of the Galápagos which reminds one of the artist Piranesi's treatment of the ruins of ancient Rome. Piranesi had a way of dwarfing his human figures and increasing the size of his buildings in such a fashion as to leave an overriding sense of the vastness of these great relics. Viewed in such perspective the present-day world appears almost trivial. In a similar fashion Melville, drawing both upon his own experience and the records of Captain Porter, has created more than a mere sketch of the islands. Captain Fitzroy of the *Beagle* once referred to the islands as "a fit shore for Pandemonium." Melville hails them as a "fallen world." It is a magnified world, like the artist Piranesi's etchings of the ruins of Rome. Viewed from the tower of the Rock Rodondo with its tiers of ravenous sea birds, the islands and their wretched inhabitants stretch into uncertain distances like a galaxy in space. The links, the connections persistently sought by critics in these sketches, lie in Melville's very emphasis upon isolation, psychological distortion and endurance. "So warped and crooked was his strange nature," Melville wrote of one hideous character, "that the very handle of his hoe seemed gradually to have shrunk and twisted in his grasp." The final sketch of the series significantly carries the title *Runaways, Castaways, Solitairies, Gravestones, Etc.* The appellations oddly reflect what might be spoken of all the bits of life which the biologist discovers upon island shores.

Over all, like some great prison tower, exerting a polarizing magnetic force, the Rock Rodondo, a "belltower" inhabited by bandit birds, suggests in a way almost demoniacal the powers loose in this abandoned world. They are the same forces grasped by Darwin under the scientifically insulating phrase "natural selection." Even he, the more conventional Victorian, once exclaimed with unaccustomed savagery, "What a book a devil's chaplain might write on the clumsy, wasteful, blundering and horribly cruel works of nature." Unconsciously he was, perhaps, anticipating the great novelist's perception of "that intangible malignity which has been from the beginning."

So far, in our account of Melville's ponderings upon his little galaxy of worlds, we have grown increasingly aware of a strange psychic gift for prefiguring symbolically in human nature some of the distortions, both beautiful and ugly, which nature allows to creep insensibly into actual existence upon solitary shores. Perhaps in the end the microcosm of the desert archipelago came to stand in Melville's mind for the world island we each inhabit. Two things, however, in this universe of his we have not yet fully examined: the giant tortoises and that "snow white angelic thing," a bird which haunts the top of Rock Rodondo.

The two most haunting symbols which occur in Melville's oceanic alphabet are the great white whale Moby Dick, and the ponderous, ungainly tortoises. Melville is far too clever a writer to define and delimit his arcane mythology. Like most true artists he is content to let his images grow and proliferate, taking such shapes as the human mind in any generation may perceive in them. It is thus that the creative genius seizes upon immortality. Generations of critics, however, have professed to see in the great whale, fate, an inexorable nature, or perhaps the very essence of an inscrutable deity. Ahab, the importunate huntsman, cries out at one point, "Be the White Whale agent, or be the White Whale principal, I will wreak [my] hate upon him." As a counterweight to this outburst, Melville interposes a subdued comment from one of the crew, "God help thee, old man, thy thoughts have created a creature in thee." Ironically, Melville has still left us in impenetrable darkness as to whether it is mankind in general or merely mad Ahab who has created "a creature."

The story of Moby Dick is not, of course, the story of the *Encantadas*. Nevertheless it is still important to understand something of the great White Whale, be he instrument or principle of fate, before we can begin to comprehend Melville's other opposing symbol of the giant tortoises or even the angelic white-winged bird that cries musically from the topmost spire of Rock Rodondo.

In *Moby Dick*, man, beating out through wintry gales and equatorial typhoons, harries the immortal whale through all the deeps of Ocean. At night its silver spoutings entice the mutilated huntsman, Ahab, who embodies the equally immortal folly, pride and grandeur of man. Yet at the moment of final disaster the previously frenzied crew, caught up hypnotically in Ahab's purposes, are released into a lost dream of home: one briefly hopes his mother has drawn his pay, another inconsequently wishes to taste cherries—cherries from the land before he dies. In the moment when the Pequod goes down, the great whale vanishes, leaving us with the inescapable impression that perhaps both the hunter and the hunt are a kind of ever-recurring dream.

If we then turn to the *Encantadas*, a work composed when Melville himself had experienced failure and derision, we find the hour of heroic confrontations such as stirred the reader of *Moby Dick* has passed. In the Galápagos amidst burnt-out volcanic vents and impenetrable thickets one creature alone seems adapted to the infernal landscape. It is not man, who seems destined inevitably to grow as distorted as the hoe wielded by the murderous creature, Oberlus. Rather it is another, a reptilian being, with an enormous instinctive will plated into a dented, iron-shelled carapace; namely, the huge Galápagos land tortoise.

These creatures, whose great bulk and individual antiquity have long impressed explorers, appear to have made a remarkable impression upon Melville's mind even when he first viewed them as a young sailor. "They seemed," he said, "newly crawled forth from beneath the foundations of the world." He was struck by their "dateless, indefinite endurance," by their astonishing ability to go without food, by healed scars upon their bodies so old that they were suggestive of geological rather than historic time. Their steadfast determination to hold to a given course despite all barriers impressed him almost as though they were the victims of a malign sorcerer. He portrays vividly the obstacles they face—splintered mountains, the metallic chasms that block their passage—and he pictures the great beasts as century after century opposing their obstinate will to the inanimate universe through which they stumble.

Melville admits, cryptically, that the tortoise has both its black and bright side. He remains fascinated by their enormous irrational persistence, which appears to revolve in his mind as a counterpoise, an act of endurance, against the equally persistent destructive principle that masked itself, or existed, in the body of the great White Whale. By contrast, volatile man frequently invited the furies that descended upon him. Unlike the tortoise he possessed "a larger capacity for degeneration." Melville here seems to be reflecting upon that steadfast patience which came to play so great a role in the autumn of his own career when, like the hoary Galápagos turtles resolutely butting their way through all encumbrances, he continued to write while the critical world slowly forgot him.

To the last the musical white bird from the top of sea-washed Rock Rodondo must have called to him. He never thought to clarify its meaning any more than he would have defined the rushing snow hill that was Moby Dick. One can only recall that another archangelic bird was dragged from heaven when the Pequod sank. It is plain that the bird was a personal symbol to Melville, some spirit voice heard above the raucous clamor of contending sea fowl. Life to Melville was clearly a mystical adventure since the day he had glimpsed the tattooed imprint of the blue shark upon a human face. He had trod as heavily as the giant tortoises upon the proprieties of his time. He had remained neither believer nor atheist, but a seeker. The falling syllables from a remote bird had been sufficient to lure him onward. Out of his life there is left only his books. From the greatest of these, *Moby Dick*, I draw the quotation from Job which, though applied to his character Ishmael, might well be Melville's own true epitaph: "I only am escaped to tell thee."

IV. CONCLUSION

The German philosopher Friederich Schlegel once commented that a work of art is finished when it is limited at every point, and yet within its border is without limitation. Certainly this observation would seem to apply to the work of the three greatest minds to visit the Galápagos, and more particularly to Charles Darwin and Herman Melville. Moreover, it is possible to consider that the islands themselves sustain Schlegel's dictum as though parts of the natural order itself, indeed perhaps the entire world of nature, fall under some comparable artistic analogy. Nature is limited at any given point of time yet, as Darwin revealed, her potentiality through time appears inexhaustible. The fauna and flora of the Galápagos Archipelago are peculiar and some of them are unique, but this uniqueness is still the product of an underlying unity. It is the working of such mysterious principles as adaptive radiation and selection which binds this assemblage of extraordinary plants and animals together and relates even the story of man to island tortoises and flightless birds.

There is a sense in which we can regard these animals as having wandered from the evolutionary road we ourselves have traveled in other potential guises. It was in this way that Darwin made sense out of what otherwise appeared to be a chaos of meaningless creations. He gave meaning to time, value to what is lost.

We are all, in fact, the product of islands, visible or invisible. At some point in the fossil past, isolation and mutation have diverted each bit of life down some solitary road from which there is no turning back. Humanity is as much the product of a figurative genetic island lost in time as is the giant Galápagos tortoise. The clever brain that so far has shielded man may prove in the end to be as vulnerable as a turtle's carapace. Nature, as the records of the past reveal, makes no promises to any form of life—least of all to life in excess of its natural limits.

Because the Galápagos had remained, until the last century, relatively untouched by settlers, there have survived upon them, into modern times, the rare and stubbornly archaic relics of a deviant and distant past. To an astute observer the shells upon the island beaches whisper more of time than of the sea's voice. The confused instincts of certain of the island birds similarly hint of continents and enemies from which they have long since escaped.

As humanity intrudes upon such isolated shores their magic is doomed to vanish as surely as from Prospero's Isle of Voices. Their exotic life has been decimated. On some islands it has already been totally extinguished by human interference. On others, more barren and less habitable, a few zoological novelties still cling to life. Islands have a way of giving protection to strange and beautiful organic forms. Nature is harsh upon the continents. There the intricate web of life is drawn ever tighter by man. Increasingly, little that is rare or exotic slips through the living mesh. The procreant darkness that normally lies concealed behind the facade of the existent world is frustrated. It ebbs away into the little shadows behind billboards, or vanishes beneath the cement of superhighways.

The natural history of the Galápagos drew attention at a fortunate moment in the history of exploration. Their peculiar inhabitants fell under observation just at a time when the old Mosaic doctrine of instantaneous creation was in the process of critical re-evaluation. A little later and these tiny evolutionary laboratories might have existed only doubtfully in the pages of forgotten logbooks.

Yet far more visibly than on the continents, such natural laboratories frequently present doorways leading into the past. Moreover, they disclose, in their singular isolation, what strange shapes can be teased from the darkness of living nature if the biological net to which we have previously referred is in any way loosened through lack of enemies. Giants, or it may be dwarfs, will peep out of hidden coverts and be found nowhere else in the world. Let a few millennia run on and stragglers on island shores will be insensibly transformed by the genetic magic hidden in their own bodies—the shape-shifting power which is the common property of all living things, and which Darwin's finches manifest so strikingly.

In the Galápagos, the finches in particular reveal this process spectacularly. Here we are dealing with a limited situation whose history, even whose intermediate forms, had survived, and were available for direct observation. By contrast the great continental worlds of life are so complex, and the evolutionary processes involved so frequently invisible, that they do not afford, to the unsophisticated, the opportunity to ask the questions which tantalized the attention of the pioneer biologists. It was not without reason, therefore, that although Darwin came to the Galápagos in quest of Tertiary fossils, his curiosity, upon stepping ashore, was soon diverted by the great tortoises which struck him as antediluvian apparitions out of an even more distant past.

William Dampier once remarked of his travels that he had "caused a map to be Ingraven, with a prick'd line, representing to the Eye the whole Thread of the Voyage at one View . . ." Though he wrote with the simple forthrightness of a navigator there is no reason, in dangerous and untracked waters, why we cannot take him, symbolically, for our guide. He recorded with equal enthusiasm everything from the size of a shark's mouth to the behavior of savages and waterspouts. He and his brother mariners had ridden the world-encircling winds of the planet. Those winds and whirling vapors had blown as freely through their heads. They had seen strange beasts shambling on untrodden shores.

West Europe, as a consequence, was quickening with new questions. The "Vast Book of the World" lay open for the reading. The solitary hermitage was no longer the source of learning. There was instead a hunger for far vistas and new worlds. The growing scientific demand for facts would in the end raise questions which could only be answered out of other waters than those the voyagers had sailed—the waters of time. It was essentially the observations made in the one, however, that would lead by the pricked line of thought to a deeper and more troubled ocean. All this we have pursued at length through the centuries that succeed Dampier. The navigator stands alone with his *Treatise on the Winds*, a pirate with a sensitive finger raised to the hint of dark, unsettling airs in a century he would never see.

It was Darwin sauntering among the burnt-out chimney stacks and sprawling reptiles of an enchanted forge, the forge of life, who saw most clearly life's inner power to transform itself. As he brooded upon the variability of the island species, with only a few miles of sea intervening between each refuge, he saw, in as yet dim perspective, that life could be as vaporous and shifting as the cloud wrack of the sea. He began to sense, moreover, that the power to change came from within, that the relaxation of the living web upon these desert islands had in some manner presented life the opportunity to creep in new, unheard-of directions. Isolation, as well as conflict, he would begin to perceive, might play a role in change. Darwin, though his theory of natural selection was not immediately devised upon those shores, would long remember the Galápagos. In his *Journal*, as we have seen, he complained wryly that it is the fate of every voyager to be hurried away from any object which has attracted his interest. Nevertheless, the memory of the islands remained and haunted him. No more than two years later, at home in London, the final synthesis to be called natural selection was achieved. In the years since, it has been strengthened and modified, until, in many minds, it affords a total explanation of the evolution of life.

Darwin was a great scientific genius, but toward the conclusion of *The Origin of Species*, for all its harsh implications, he could not resist adding a complacent line of Victorian sentiment; namely, that out of the eternal warfare of nature "all corporeal . . . endowments will tend to progress toward perfection." Melville was, in his own way, if not a scientist, then at least a sturdier, less satisfied searcher. "Will we ever stop changing?" he once asked. In his heart he already knew the answer. It drove him finally to the Holy Land to peer into an empty sepulchre and grope among the refuse of creation. He will not give over, observed his friend Hawthorne, but suffers, and wanders to and fro in sandy deserts. He returned from Palestine to fall silent except to remark cryptically that Judea was one accumulation of stones.

It was close upon the time of that despairing journey that Melville ironically renewed the everlasting yea of life in the unswerving march of the giant tortoises. To the discerning eye they lie across his final work as moving and eternal as the great White Whale. And so they are, for they assert the most important missing ingredient in Dar-

win's Empire of Accident. However we may choose to phrase it, they assert the will, the driving force of life which Darwin does not attempt to explain but without which the great beast of the world would lie stricken and silent with all its parts undone.

The Encantadas are not some dying degenerate murmur from a once great writer. Rather the march of the turtles represents another and as profound a symbol as the whale that vanquished the Pequod and her captain. The White Whale has been called fate, "he who breaks everything and is not conquered." But where fate exists there must be equally the affirmation of defiance, the indeterminacy of escape which we call life. Somehow that will is embodied in our living substance. The spout of the White Whale in all meridians is no more mysterious than the inexorable blundering progress of the elephantine turtles through Melville's belittered universe. If the white whale embodies ruin, the armored turtles, like those of Oriental lore, "uphold the universal cope." The alternating assertion and negation of life revolved perpetually in Melville's brain as surely as the spinning maelstrom that engulfed the Pequod. In contrast to his spokesman Ishmael there was for Melville no release from his torment. In the words of one biographer he sank into death without a ripple of renown, lost from the sight of his generation far out in the great waters.

In lieu of treasure Dampier and his compatriots had felt upon their brows the morning winds of the planet. Darwin, the Victorian scientist, had glimpsed a sufficient bit of what he termed the "infernal regions" to weld them into the fabric of a world-shaking hypothesis and proceed homeward to universal fame. Melville, the artist, had alone, like Ahab, challenged the immortal whale and suffered, in his writing career, the total wreck that was the Pequod's fate.

Perhaps in the end his observation that "truth comes in with darkness" marks a profundity to which Dampier's Ingraven chart still leads, but the "prick'd line" grows, like all the maps of buccaneers and treasure seekers, increasingly difficult to follow. Nor is the way made easier when Melville adds an innocent commentary which seems to partake, as do almost all of Melville's lines, of something hidden, some mocking ambiguous instruction neglected to our peril. "Never heed," he writes, "yonder Burnt District of the Enchanted Isles. Look edgeways past them to the south." But in so looking we are gazing where all meridians converge upon the Southern Pole. We have come upon the bane of mariners, the navigation from fire to ice, from past to future where all needles spin.

I have said earlier that in the Enchanted Isles anchors

had a way of slipping. I do not think the story begun there is yet completed. A few months ago after a lengthy chat I asked a scientist of international repute, surrounded in his cluttered office by scattered specimens and offshore charts, what he thought of the islands. He paused, removed his pipe and stared into space so long that I began to entertain doubts that he had heard me. Finally, however, he nodded and spoke slowly, looking beyond and quite through me as though at some other place. Unknowingly the words he spoke echoed from another century. "Each island," he said carefully, more to himself than to me, "is a very beautiful and different hell." Melville, I thought, would have understood this man. I did not ask for the longitude I had come to inquire about. I picked up my hat and went away quietly, leaving him staring, unseeing, at some strange creature in a bottle. —LOREN EISELEY

BIBLIOGRAPHY

Anonymous, "Geographical Distribution of Animals," *The Edinburgh Review*, Vol. 53 (1831), pp. 328-360.

Anonymous, "Voyages of Captains King and Fitzroy," *The Edinburgh Review*, Vol. 69 (1839), pp. 467-493.

Barlow, Nora, *Charles Darwin and the Voyage of the Beagle*, New York, Philosophical Library, 1946.

Bevington, Merle M., *The Saturday Review, 1855-1868*, New York, Columbia University Press, 1941.

Blyth, Edward, "An Attempt to Classify the Variations of Animals, etc.," *Magazine of Natural History*, Vol. 8 (1835), pp. 40-53.

—— "On the Psychological Distinctions Between Man and All Other Animals, etc.," *Magazine of Natural History*, Vol. 1 N.S. (1837), Parts I, II, III.

Bowman, Robert L. (ed.), *The Galápagos*, Berkeley, University of California Press, 1966.

Carlquist, Sherwin, *Island Life: A Natural History of the Islands of the World*, Garden City, New York, Natural History Press, 1965.

Cawley, Robert Ralston, *Unpathed Waters: Studies in the Influence of the Voyagers on Elizabethan Literature*, New York, Octagon Books, Inc., 1967.

Cuvier, Georges Baron, "Historical Eloge of the late Sir Joseph Banks, Baronet, President of the Royal Society," *The Edinburgh New Philosphical Journal*, Vol. 2 (1826), pp. 1-22.

Eiseley, Loren, "Charles Darwin, Edward Blyth and the Theory of Natural Selection," *Proceedings of the American Philosophical Society*, Vol. 103 (1959), pp. 94-158.

—— "Darwin, the Human Being, the Adventurer in Ideas," *New York Herald Tribune Book Review*, June 14, 1959, pp. 1 & 11.

—— "Darwin, Coleridge, and the Theory of Unconscious Creation," *Daedalus*, Vol. 94 (Summer, 1965), pp. 588-602.

—— "Charles Lyell," *Scientific American*, Vol. 201 (1959), pp. 98-101.

Fogle, Richard Harter, *Melville's Shorter Tales*, Norman, Oklahoma, University of Oklahoma Press, 1960.

Franklin, H. Bruce, *The Wake of the Gods: Melville's Mythology*, Stanford, Stanford University Press, 1963.

Frantz, Ray W., *The English Traveller and the Movement of Ideas, 1660-1732*, Lincoln, University of Nebraska Press, 1967.

Gleim, William S., *The Meaning of Moby Dick*, New York, Russell and Russell, 1962.

Grant, Robert E., "General View of the Characters and the Distribution of Extinct Animals," *British Annual and Epitome of the Progress of Science for 1839*, ed. by Robert D. Thomson, London, 1838.

Hofsten, Nils, "Zur alteren Geschichte des Diskontinuitats problems in der Biogeographie," Zoologische Annalen, Vol. 7 (1919), pp. 197-353.

MacArthur, R. H. and E. O. Wilson, *Island Biogeography*, Princeton, Princeton University Press, 1967.

Melville, Herman, The Shorter Novels of Herman Melville (Including *The Encantadas, or Enchanted Isles*), edited with an introduction by Raymond Weaver, Fawcett Publications, New York, 1967.

Morton, Samuel G., "Doctrine of Specific Organic Centres," *The Edinburgh New Philosophical Journal*, Vol. 51 (1851), pp. 197-198.

Nelson, Bryan, *Galapagos: Islands of Birds*, London, Longmans, Green and Co., 1968.

Porter, David, *Journal of a Cruise Made To the Pacific Ocean in the United States Frigate Essex in the Years 1812, 1813 and 1814*, Philadelphia, Bradford and Inskeep, 1815.

Ritchie, James, "The Edinburgh Explorers," *University of Edinburgh Journal*, Vol. 12, (1943), pp. 155-159.

—— "Evolution and the Galapagos Islands," *University of Edinburgh Journal*, Vol. 12 (1943), pp. 97-105.

Ritter, William E., "Mechanical Ideas In the Last Hundred Years of Biology," *American Naturalist*, Vol. 72 (1938), pp. 315-323.

Shipman, Joseph C., *William Dampier: Seaman-Scientist*, Lawrence, University of Kansas Library Series No. 15, 1962.

Slevin, Joseph Richard, "The Galápagos Islands: a History of Their Exploration," *Occasional Papers of the California Academy of Sciences*, No. XXV, San Francisco, 1959.

Strickland, H. G. and G. A. Melville, *The Dodo and Its Kindred*, London, Reeves, 1843.

Vincent, Howard P., *The Trying-Out of Moby Dick*, Carbondale, Southern Illinois University Press, 1949.

West, Geoffrey, *Charles Darwin*, New Haven, Yale University Press, 1938.

Wildenow, D. C., *The Principles of Botany and of Vegetable Physiology*, London, 1811.

Young, J. Z., "The Darwin Centenary," *New Statesman* (March 15, 1958), pp. 337-338.

Ziswiller, Vinzenz, *Extinct and Vanishing Animals*, New York, Springer-Verlag, 1967.

ABINGDON
(Pinta)

BINDLOE
(Marchena)

TOWER
(Genovesa)

Darwin Bay

Roca Redondo

Point Albemarle

Cape
Berkeley

Banks Bay

Punta Espinosa

JAMES
(Santiago)

James Bay

BARTHOLOMEW
(Bartholomé)

Urvina Bay

JERVIS
(Rábida)

N. SEYMOUR

S. SEYMOUR
(Baltra)

NARBOROUGH
(Fernandina)

Cartago Bay

Conway Bay

Elizabeth Bay

Plaza

DUNCAN
(Pinzón)

INDEFATIGABLE
(Santa Cruz)

CHATHAM
(San Cristóbal)

ALBEMARLE (Isabela)

Point
Pitt

CROSSMAN
(Los Hermanos)

Academy Bay

BARRINGTON
(Santa Fe)

Wreck Bay

Iguana Cove

Villamil

Freshwater Bay

BRATTLE
(Tortuga)

Hancock Bank

Macgowen Reef

Post Office Bay

Black Beach

CHARLES
(Floreana)

GARDNER-near-Charles

GARDNER-near-Hood

HOOD
(Española)

This Island I called the Duke of York's Island: there lying to the Eastward of that
(a fine round Island) which I called the Duke of Norfolk's Island. And to the
Westward of the Duke of York's Island, lieth another curious Island, which I called
the Duke of Albemarle's; in which is a commodious Bay or Harbour, where you
may ride Landlock'd: And before the sad Bay lieth another Island, the which I called
Sir John Narborough's: And between York and Albemarle's Island lieth a small one,
which my fancy led me to call Cowley's enchanted Island; for we having had a sight of
it upon several points of the Compass, it appear'd always in many different Forms,
sometimes like a ruined Fortification; upon another Point, like a great City . . .

1. CORSAIRS

A wonderful thing about islands is their capacity for discovery. They can be discovered, rediscovered, and rediscovered again, yet still seem virgin ground. Nowhere is it easier to imagine yourself the first than alone on a desert island in the center of a blue sea. The Galápagos Islands, in spite of their long human history, are virgin islands. Large areas of their interiors are unexplored, and in those regions that are known lava, cactus and thorn resist the marks of man. On certain great lava fields, clearly late-risen from the sea, one feels himself not just the first human to venture, but the first living thing, the first emissary of life.

The first men familiar with the Galápagos, the buccaneers, were men whose lives were spent rounding strange continents, pursuing strange beasts through strange jungles, encountering strange peoples—men to whom discovery was a daily affair. Their journals are filled with names that must have puzzled or frightened their countrymen. Names of places: Tonquin, Tenan, Cachao and Achin, Bencouli, Campeachy, Mindanao and Teneriffe, the Bashee Islands, the Isle of Queriso, Sam Shu and Hoc Shu. Names of creatures: manatees, squashes, tigre-cats, gally-wasps, waree and centapees; whiprays, rasprays and gar-fish. There were melory trees and tar trees; cockrecoes, bill-birds, quams, Correscoes, Subtle-Jacks and humming-birds. The buccaneers surely would have agreed to a man that, as Thoreau would later write, "nothing but the wildest imagination can conceive of the manner of life we are living. Nature is a wizard." They lived a perpetual, involuntary childhood in which new smells, colors, sounds, visions, horizons and winds came at them with each new day.

And yet the buccaneers were excited in their discovery of the Galápagos. The islands were desert, but the buccaneers had acquired a taste for desert spaces. The island beasts were not as spectacular as the beasts of the mainland—the iguanas not nearly so brilliantly colored as their jungle cousins to the east—but there was something in their primitiveness, in the austerity of their situation, that stirred the pirates.

Today, three hundred years later, the same qualities stir us. Our good fortune, so good only the wildest imagination could hope for it, is that we can row through the same surf, jump into the same clear water, and pull our boats high on the same hard white sand that Captains Dampier, Davis, Cowley and Woodes Rogers beached on, and find the same unknown island at our feet.

Wee lay at Lobus above eight and forty houres, and knowing that wee had more than an hundred prisoners on board not knowing where to gett water, nor where to find a place of making a Magazeene for flower but that wee should be hunted out and have our flower destroyed, wee sailed away to the Westward to see if wee could find those Islands called the Galipoloes, which made the Spaniards laugh at us telling us they were Inchanted Islands, and that there was never any but one Captaine Porialto that had ever seene them, but would not come neare them to Anchor to them, and that they were but shadowes and noe reall Islands.

. . .

June 1684:

About the beginning of this Month wee saw an Island on our Starboard side making high Land and Low Land, being a very likely Island to have water, upon being well Repleinshed with wood, but by reason of the strong Current that runneth there wee could not fetch it, That Island I named King Charles the Seconds Island, by my Judgement it lyeth in the Latitude of one South Latitude and Thirty Minutes—Longitude two hundred and seaventy eight Degrees and fifty minutes standing still to the Westward I saw severall Islands, but that which I liked best, I came to Anchor under in a good Bay having seaven fathom water, there being upon this Island to the South end a good Harbor for many Shipps to ride, I beleive his Majestyes Navy might ride there in safety, wee put the Boat a shoare, but found no water there but wee found Land Turtle very great, and Sea turtle very good and large and great plenty, and a sort of ffowles called fflemingo with Goanoes, which our men brought aboard, the small Birds being not in the least possessed with feare, they lighted on our mens heads and Armes and they tooke them off, which at first seemed strange to me but I did the same my selfe after that.

. . .

Withall, but I cannot say how farr his Majestyes Island stretcheth away

to the South East, by reason that most of those Islands having had sulphurous

matter that hath sett them on fire, they have beene burned formerly,

and some parts of them blowne up, the Land and Rocks or some of them

are lying in soe much Confusion that there is no Travelling on them,

the Land that has beene burnt seemed like to Cindars, but very heavy, which

made me thinke they were mixt with some mettall, for the Mother of

Mettalls is here in great plenty upon this Iland which they say is Brimstone.

. . .

Cinder slope, Buccaneer Cove, James Island

Wee were sailing along the Duke of Albemarles Island, the sun shineing
made us thinke our hill had been coverd with Gold, when wee came to see it,
it was fine Brimstone as fine as flower.

—EDWARD DAVIS

While the *Bachelor's Delight* was within the Galápagos, and while Captain Cook was recovering, Ambrosia Cowley took time to chart and name the Galápagos Islands. The naming was a singular procedure, for they were named after the nominal enemies of the English buccaneers. I say 'nominal enemies,' for it was supposedly English policy to co-operate with Spain in the punishment of the buccaneers. Some of the islands were named in honour of the English officials at Nassau and Bermuda, who had instructions from Charles II of England that piracy was to be rigorously suppressed. Spain had complained vigorously to the English that the depredations of English privateers were countenanced by the English crown, and while thus officially England was not at war with Spain, its decrees against piracy were only half-heartedly carried out by the British officials at Jamaica. They constantly closed one eye to the piratical action of their countrymen, and at times both eyes.

For the lax enforcement of law by this group of men Cowley showed his gratitude by honouring them with islands in the Galápagos bearing their names. Wainman (called Wenman) and Brattle were named after Lords Wainman and Nicholas Brattle, and Bindloe after Colonel Robert Bindloss, who was a member of the Council of Jamaica and the brother-in-law of Henry Morgan; perhaps the buccaneers had reason to remember him kindly. . . .

The largest island of the archipelago was named, curiously enough, not for the reigning monarch, but for the 'King Maker,' George Monk, First Duke of Albemarle, the general who had restored Charles II to the throne. He was thus honoured because of his policy toward the buccaneers. The Duke had arrived in Jamaica in 1687 and at once allied himself with the searovers, even reappointing Sir Henry Morgan and Colonel Bindloss to the Council from which office they had both been suspended. The large island west of Albemarle was called after Sir John Narborough, Samuel Pepys' own protégé, the celebrated navigator who, in the year 1669, was dispatched by the Admiralty in His Majesty's ship *Sweepstakes*, on a voyage to the South Seas, partly commercial and partly exploratory.

The small island between James and Indefatigable, Cowley named Sir Anthony Dean's Island, after the shipbuilder to Charles II. This gentleman, it will be remembered, was incarcerated in London Tower with Samuel Pepys for certain practices with regard to booty taken during battle. . . .

Off the western coast of Indefatigable are three small islets that Cowley called Guy Fawkes, after the man who tried to blow up Parliament.

—VICTOR WOLFGANG VON HAGEN

Green Heron, Santa Cruz Island

Near two centuries ago Barrington Isle was the resort of that famous wing of the West Indian Buccaneers, which, upon their repulse from the Cuban waters, crossing the Isthmus of Darien, ravaged the Pacific side of the Spanish colonies, and, with the regularity and timing of a modern mail, waylaid the royal treasure ships plying between Manilla and Acapulco. After the toils of piratic war, here they came to say their prayers, enjoy their free-and-easies, count their crackers from the cask, their doubloons from the keg, and measure their silks of Asia with long Toledos for their yard-sticks. . . .

"I once landed on its western side," says a sentimental voyager long ago, "where it faces the black buttress of Albemarle. I walked beneath groves of trees; not very lofty, and not palm trees, or orange trees, or peach trees, to be sure; but for all that, after long sea-faring very beautiful to walk under, even though they supplied no fruit. And here, in calm spaces at the heads of glades, and on the shaded tops of slopes commanding the most quiet scenery—what do you think I saw? Seats which might have served Brahmins and presidents of peace societies. Fine old ruins of what had once been symmetric lounges of stone and turf; they bore every mark both of artificialness and age, and were undoubtedly made by the Buccaneers. One had been a long sofa, with back and arms, just such a sofa as the poet Gray might have loved to throw himself upon, his Crebillon in hand.

"Though they sometimes tarried here for months at a time, and used the spot for a storing-place for spare spars, sails, and casks; yet it is highly improbable that the buccaneers ever erected dwelling-houses upon the isle. They never were here except their ships remained, and they would most likely have slept on board. I mention this, because I cannot avoid the thought that it is hard to impute the construction of these romantic seats to any other motive than one of pure peacefulness and kindly fellowship with nature. That the buccaneers perpetrated the greatest outrages is very true; that some of them were mere cut-throats is not to be denied; but we know that here and there among their host was a Dampier, a Wafer, and a Cowley, and likewise other men, whose worst reproach was their desperate fortunes; whom persecution, or adversity, or secret and unavengeable wrongs, had driven from Christian society to seek the melancholy solitude or the guilty adventures of the sea.

. . .

"But during my ramble on the isle I was not long in discovering other tokens, of things quite in accordance with those wild traits, popularly—and no doubt truly enough—imputed to the freebooters at large. Had I picked up old sails and rusty hoops I would only have thought of the ship's carpenter and cooper. But I found old cutlasses and daggers reduced to mere threads of rust, which doubtless had stuck between Spanish ribs ere now. These were signs of the murderer and robber; the reveller likewise had left his trace. Mixed with shells, fragments of broken jars were lying here and there, high up upon the beach. They were precisely like the jars now used upon the Spanish coast for the wine and Pisco spirits of that country.

"With a rusty dagger-fragment in one hand, and a bit of a wine-jar in another, I sat me down on the ruinous green sofa I have spoken of, and bethought me long and deeply of these same buccaneers. Could it be possible, that they robbed and murdered one day, revelled the next, and rested themselves by turning meditative philosophers, rural poets, and seat-builders on the third? Not very improbable, after all. For consider the vacillations of a man. Still, strange as it may seem, I must also abide by the more charitable thought; namely, that among these adventurers were some gentlemanly, companionable souls, capable of genuine tranquillity and virtue."

—SALVATOR R. TARNMOOR

2. SAILORS

As buccaneers left Galápagos waters in the early eighteenth century, they were replaced by a more common kind of seaman. Whaling ships, occasional warships, and ships on voyages of exploration stopped at the Islands. Sailors went ashore in search of water and of tortoises, and on coming back they recorded what they had seen of a new land. What is striking in the sailors' accounts is the simplicity and freshness of their vision of the Islands. They did not view the Galápagos as darkly as Bishop Berlanga had—they were not thirsty and lost; or as gratefully as the buccaneers had—there were no Spaniards after them. They were excited by the strange animals, they wondered at the terrain, they appreciated everything after long months at sea, and then they departed. Of them all, only Herman Melville tried to make something momentous of the Islands. The sailors were as yet innocent of how the Islands were tied up with their ancestry. No one after Darwin would be able to look on the Islands so easily and with such light hearts.

The "guaner" is a singular creature of the lizard tribe—resembling the chameleon in shape and size. It is about a foot and a half long, black, with a serrated ridge along the back and tail. Take him by the "narrative" and he will hang to the honey-combed rocks like a cat to the carpet; nor can you injure his head piece by striking it against a stone for a half hour together. Pelt him, and he will poke his nose under shelter, nor budge from his position though an hundred missiles strike his exposed body. We caught two, and after killing them at least a dozen times apiece, we put them in the boat— as they are said to make an excellent soup. But, alas for our expected treat— on looking for them ten minutes afterwards, they had scaled the walls of their prison, and were nowhere to be found!

—C.T.H.

On the fifth day out from Paita, the cheerful cry of "land ho" rang merrily from our mast-head, and soon the undulating outline of Chatham was dimly visible in the distance. About noon we were abreast of the southwest corner of the island, a point designated on our charts as the best landing place. But as our Captain was unacquainted with the vicinity, and numerous evidences of sunken reefs were apparent, he would not risk too near an approach with the vessel. At about one o'clock, P.M., therefore, the yawl was lowered, and with a full crew, ourself and partner in the stern sheets, a bottle of pisco, and "grub" enough for a couple of meals, we pulled heartily for the entrance of a kind of cove, distant about three miles, and defended by an ugly looking line of breakers to seaward. Capt. B. had been instructed to "lay to" until nightfall, when if we did not intend to return, we would light a fire, and he could stand off shore during the night, returning for us in the morning. With a smooth sea, and the prospect of a scramble over the unknown hills of a desert island, our men pulled lustily for the cove, and after some pretty careful navigation among the sunken rocks and "niggerheads" that made off from the reef, and a smart drenching from a big roller as we touched the beach, we at last effected a safe landing. Finding the tide had fallen about four feet below high water mark, and not knowing whether it were rising or falling, we took the precaution to haul our heavy boat high and dry on the beach, and having made all snug in case the tide were rising, away we started like uncaged birds, each bent on having a "good time" even though we should fail to find opportunity for the classic amusement of "backing down terrapins."

Oh! the exhilaration of such an excursion to the pent up passenger at sea! It is exciting to make port anywhere after a long passage on the briny waves, but there is in the first sight of an uninhabited island a charm to the young voyager, greater far than that of landing at the crowded throughfares of commerce. You think of Crusoe and Selkirk. You are monarch of all you survey. For you alone of your race, do the winds blow, the trees vegitate, the waves whiten the beach. You fancy yourself a miniature Columbus, and discoverer-like,—you feel—no it is we in this instance— like jotting down all your observations, that when you return to the abodes of life you may add your mite to the geographical knowledge of those poor unfortunates whose travels have not led them so far from home.

—C.T.H.

Young Opuntia, San Cristóbal Island

Under one we saw a very large male terrapin, far above our ability to carry,
and on looking a little farther, we found almost under every tree one of the
same kind. These huge creatures sat unconcerned, and it was our impression
that they had been here for the last five hundred years. When disturbed,
they draw in their feet, drop their lower shell on the ground and make a
hissing noise not unlike a snake. They do not offer to bite, neither
will they run. Some of them were eating cabbage leaves, which had fallen
from the trees. Here again how wonderful are the arrangements of Him
who provides food, but few facilities for obtaining food, neither being
able to climb trees, or to kill other animals, so slow is their motion.
Under these trees, which afford them comfortable shade, they rest,
watching the fall of a leaf, and when it falls they eat it. If one should not
fall for a month, why, he could remain without eating.

—CAMILLAS

Opuntia trunks, Santa Cruz Island

February 14th. On Monday the fourteenth, at two o'clock, A.M. while the sable mantle of night was yet spread over the mighty Pacific, shrouding the neighbouring islands from our view, and while the stillness of death reigned everywhere about us, our ears were suddenly assailed by a sound that could only be equalled by ten thousand thunders bursting upon the air at once; while, at the same instant, the whole hemisphere was lighted up with a horrid glare that might have appalled the stoutest heart! I soon ascertained that one of the volcanoes of Narborough Island, which had quietly slept for the last ten years, had suddenly broken forth with accumulated vengeance. . . .

Had it been the "crack of doom" that aroused them, my men could not have been sooner on deck, where they stood gazing like 'sheeted spectres,' speechless and bewildered with astonishment and dismay. The heavens appeared to be one blaze of fire, intermingled with millions of falling stars and meteors; while the flames shot upward from the peak of Narborough to the height of at least two thousand feet in air. All hands soon became sensible of the cause of the startling phenomenon, and on recovering from their first panic could contemplate its progress with some degree of composure. . . .

A river of melted lava was now seen rushing down the side of the mountain, pursuing a serpentine course to the sea, a distance of about three miles from the blazing orifice of the volcano. This dazzling stream descended in a gully, one-fourth of a mile in width, presenting the appearance of a tremendous torrent of melted iron running from the furnace. Although the mountain was steep, and the gully capacious, the flaming river could not descend with sufficient rapidity to prevent its overflowing its banks in certain places, and forming new rivers, which branched out in almost every direction, each rushing downward as if eager to cool its temperament in the deep caverns of the neighbouring ocean. The demon of fire seemed rushing to the embraces of Neptune; and dreadful indeed was the uproar occasioned by their meeting. The ocean boiled and roared and bellowed, as if a civil war had broken out in the Tartarean gulf.

. . .

Flightless cormorants and lava, Punta Espinosa
(a point formed by the eruption described above)

At three A.M., I ascertained the temperature of the water, by Fahrenheit's thermometer, to be 61°, while that of the air was 71°. At eleven A.M., the air was 113°, and the water 100°, the eruption still continuing with unabated fury. The *Tartar's* anchorage was about ten miles to the northward of the mountain, and the heat was so great that the melted pitch was running from the vessel's seams, and the tar dropping from the rigging. . . .

Our situation was every hour becoming more critical and alarming. Not a breath of air was stirring to fill a sail, had we attempted to escape; so that we were compelled to remain idle and unwilling spectators of a pyrotechnic exhibition which evinced no indications of even a temporary suspension. All that day the fires continued to rage with unabating activity, while the mountain still continued to belch forth its melted entrails in an unceasing cataract.

The mercury continued to rise till four P.M., when the temperature of the air had increased to 123°, and that of the water to 105°. Our respiration now became difficult, and several of the crew complained of extreme faintness. It was evident that something must be done and that promptly. "O for a cap-full of wind!" was the prayer of each. The breath of a light zephyr from the continent, scarcely perceptible to the cheek, was at length announced as the welcome signal for the word, "All hands, unmoor!" This was a little before eight P.M. The anchor was soon apeak, and every inch of canvass extended along the spars, where it hung in useless drapery.

All was again suspense and anxious expectation. Again the zephyr breathed and hope revived. At length it was announced from aloft that the lighter canvass began to feel the air; and in a few minutes more the topsails began gradually to fill, when the anchor was brought to the bow, and the *Tartar* began to move. At eight o'clock we were wafted by a fine little easterly breeze, for which we felt grateful to Heaven.

. . .

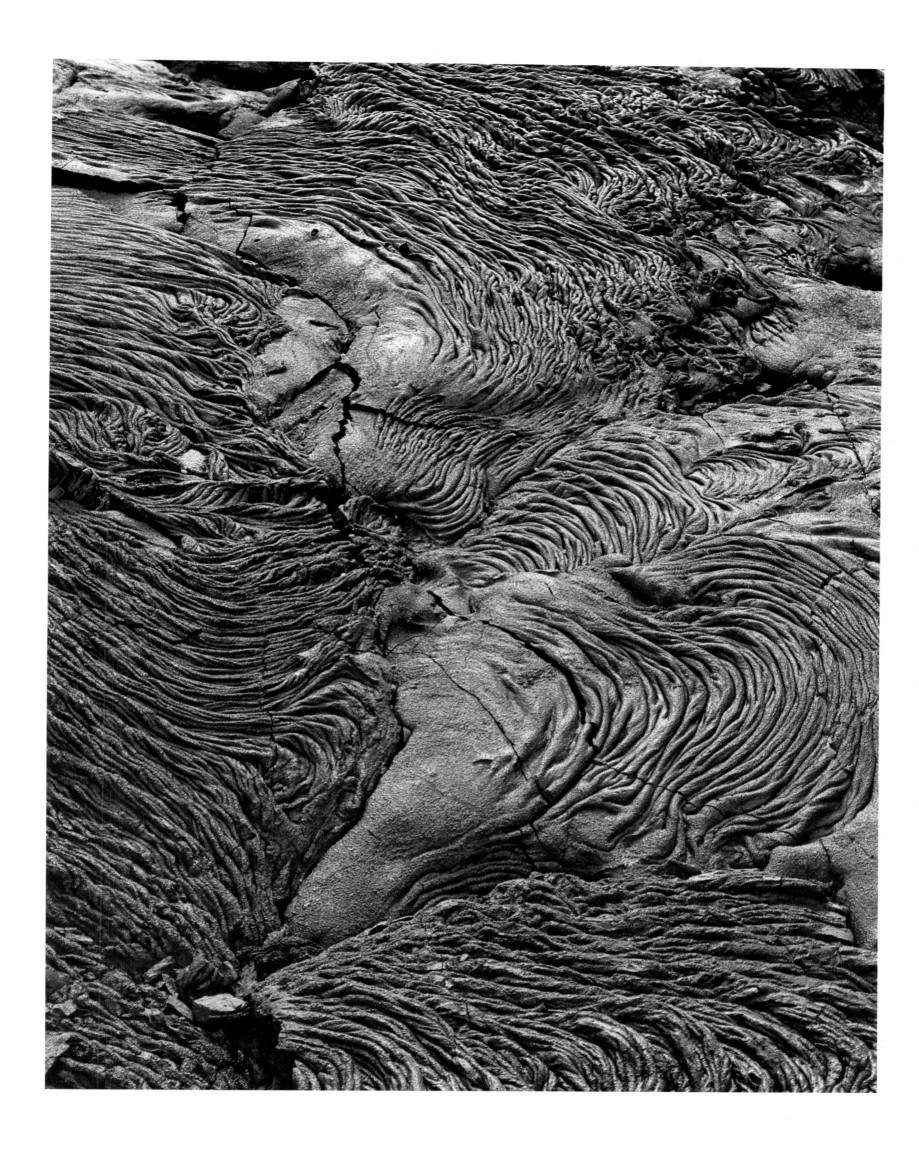

Our course lay southward, through the little strait or sound that separated the burning mountain from Albemarle Island; my object being to get to windward of Narborough as soon as possible. It is true that the northwest passage from Banks's Bay, by Cape Berkley, would have been a shorter route to the main ocean; but not the safest, under existing circumstances. I therefore chose to run south, to Elizabeth Bay, though in doing so we had to pass within about four miles of those rivers of flaming lava, which were pouring into the waters of the bay. Had I adopted the other course, and passed to the leeward of Narborough, we might have got clear of the island, but it would have been impossible to prevent the sails and rigging taking fire; as the whole atmosphere on the lee side of the bay appeared to be one mass of flame. The deafening sounds accompanying the eruption still continued; indeed the terrific grandeur of the scene would have been incomplete without it.

Heaven continued to favour us with a fine breeze, and the *Tartar* slid along through the almost boiling ocean at the rate of about seven miles an hour. On passing the currents of melted lava, I became apprehensive that I should lose some of my men, as the influence of the heat was so great that several of them were incapable of standing. At that time the mercury in the thermometer was at 147° but on immersing it in water, it instantly rose to 150°. Had the wind deserted us here, the consequences must have been horrible. But the mercy of Providence was still extended toward us—the refreshing breeze still urged us forward towards a more temperate atmosphere; so that at eleven P.M. we were safely anchored at the south extremity of the bay, while the flaming Narborough lay fifteen miles to the leeward.

Here the temperature of the air was 110°, and that of the water 102°; but at eight o'clock the next morning, the 16th, there being no abatement in the rage of the vomiting volcano, the heat had increased to such an alarming degree that we found it necessary again to get under way and abandon the bay entirely.

—BENJAMIN MORRELL

Marine iguanas, Punta Espinosa

HERMAN MELVILLE

Herman Melville touched on the Galápagos as a young man, but never really got into the Islands until much later. He returned to them from a distance, but not by sea. Stranded in New York by family and responsibility, and a little old to resume the sea life anyway, Melville rebuilt the Islands in his head and set them down on paper. He used the library, but chiefly relied on his memory, and on his genius at making the ocean and all salty creation real.

He remembered tortoises on the deck at night in the light of his lantern, and realized that he had seen more than tortoises. He described what he had seen and it became part of the second sketch of *The Encantadas*. He read of General José Villamil, the founder of a colony on Charles Island, he improved the story a bit and it became the seventh sketch, "Charles's Isle and the Dog-King."

The old memory of the Enchanted Isles, the idea of them, was all that Melville needed. They were for him islands in what Wallace Stegner calls the geography of Hope.

. . . Nor even at the risk of meriting the charge of absurdly believing in enchantments, can I restrain the admission that sometimes, even now, when leaving the crowded city to wander out July and August among the Adirondack Mountains, far from the influences of towns and proportionally nigh to the mysterious ones of Nature; when at such times I sit me down in the mossy head of some deep-wooded gorge, surrounded by prostrate trunks of blasted pines, and recall, as in a dream, my other and far-distant rovings in the baked heart of the charmed isles; and remember the sudden glimpses of dusky shells, and long languid necks protruded from the leafless thickets; and again have beheld the vitreous inland rocks worn down and grooved into deep ruts by ages and ages of the slow draggings of tortoises in quest of pools of scanty water; I can hardly resist the feeling that in my time I have indeed slept upon evilly enchanted ground.

Nay, such is the vividness of my memory, or the magic of my fancy, that I know not whether I am not the occasional victim of optical delusion concerning the Gallipagos. For often in scenes of social merriment, and especially at revels held by candle light in old-fashioned mansions— when the shadows are thrown into the further recesses of an angular and spacious room, making them put on a look of haunted undergrowth of lonely woods—I have drawn the attention of my comrades by my fixed gaze and sudden change of air, as I have seemed to see, slowly emerging from those imagined solitudes, and heavily crawling along the floor, the ghost of a gigantic tortoise, with "Memento . . ." burning in live letters upon his back.

. . .

Take five-and-twenty heaps of cinders dumped here and there in an outside city lot; imagine some of them magnified into mountains, and the vacant lot the sea; and you will have a fit idea of the general aspect of the Encantadas, or Enchanted Isles. A group rather of extinct volcanoes than of isles; looking much as the world at large might, after a penal conflagration.

It is to be doubted whether any spot of earth can, in desolateness, furnish a parallel to this group. Abandoned cemeteries of long ago, old cities by piecemeal tumbling to their ruin, these are melancholy enough; but, like all else which has but once been associated with humanity they still awaken in us some thoughts of sympathy, however sad. Hence, even the Dead Sea, along with whatever other emotions it may at times inspire, does not fail to touch in the pilgrim some of his less unpleasurable feelings.

And as for solitariness; the great forests of the north, the expanses of unnavigated waters, the Greenland ice-fields, are the profoundest of solitudes to a human observer; still the magic of their changeable tides and seasons mitigates their terror, because, though unvisited by men, those forests are visited by the May; the remotest seas reflect familiar stars even as Lake Erie does; and in the clear air of a fine Polar day, the irradiated, azure ice shows beautifully as malachite.

But the special curse, as one may call it, of the Encantadas, that which exalts them in desolation above Idumea and the Pole, is that to them change never comes; neither the change of seasons nor of sorrows. Cut by the Equator, they know not autumn and they know not spring; while already reduced to the lees of fire, ruin itself can work little more upon them. The showers refresh the deserts, but in these isles, rain never falls. Like split Syrian gourds, left withering in the sun, they are cracked by an everlasting drought beneath a torrid sky. "Have mercy upon me," the wailing spirit of the Encantadas seems to cry, "and send Lazarus that he may dip the tip of his finger in water and cool my tongue, for I am tormented in this flame."

· · ·

Another feature in these isles is their emphatic uninhabitableness. It is deemed a fit type of all-forsaken overthrow, that the jackal should den in the wastes of weedy Babylon; but the Encantadas refuse to harbour even the outcasts of the beasts. Man and wolf alike disown them. Little but reptile life is here found:—tortoises, lizards, immense spiders, snakes, and the strangest anomaly of outlandish Nature, the aguano. No voice, no low, no howl is heard; the chief sound of life here is a hiss.

. . .

On most of the isles where vegetation is found at all, it is more ungrateful that the blankness of Aracama. Tangled thickets of wiry bushes, without fruit and without a name, springing up among deep fissures of calcined rock, and treacherously masking them; or a parched growth of distorted cactus trees.

In many places the coast is rock-bound, or more properly, clinker-bound; tumbled masses of blackish or greenish stuff like the dross of an iron-furnace, forming dark clefts and caves here and there, into which a ceaseless sea pours a fury of foam; overhanging them with a swirl of grey, haggard mist, amidst which sail screaming flights of unearthly birds heightening the dismal din. However calm the sea without, there is no rest for these swells and those rocks, they lash and are lashed, even when the outer ocean is most at peace with itself. On the oppressive, clouded days such as are peculiar to this part of the watery Equator, the dark vitrified masses, many of which raise themselves among white whirlpools and breakers in detached and perilous places off the shore, present a most Plutonian sight. In no world but a fallen one could such lands exist.

. . .

If now you desire the population of Albemarle, I will give you, in round
numbers, the statistics, according to the most reliable estimates
made upon the spot:

Men	none
Ant-eaters	unknown
Man-haters	unknown
Lizards	500,000
Snakes	500,000
Spiders	10,000,000
Salamanders	unknown
Devils	do.
Making a clean total of	11,000,000

exclusive of an incomputable host of fiends, ant-eaters, man-haters,
and salamanders.

. . .

Nor would the appellation, enchanted, seem misapplied in still another sense. For concerning the peculiar reptile inhabitant of these wilds —whose presence gives the group its second Spanish name, Gallipagos —concerning the tortoises found here, most mariners have long cherished a superstition, not more frightful than grotesque. They earnestly believe that all wrecked sea-officers, more especially commodores and captains, are at death (and in some cases, before death) transformed into tortoises; thenceforth dwelling upon these hot aridities, sole solitary Lords of Asphaltum.

. . .

Sea lions, Hood Island

It was after sunset when the adventurers returned. I looked down over
the ship's high side as if looking down over the curb of a well, and dimly
saw the damp boat deep in the sea with some unwonted weight. Ropes were
dropped over, and presently three huge antediluvian-looking tortoises,
after much straining, were landed on deck. They seemed hardly of the seed
of earth. We had been abroad upon the waters for five long months,
a period amply sufficient to make all things of the land wear a fabulous
hue to the dreamy mind. Had three Spanish custom-house officers boarded
us then, it is not unlikely that I should have curiously stared at them,
felt of them, and stroked them much as savages observe civilized guests.
But instead of three custom-house officers, behold these really wondrous
tortoises—none of your schoolboy mud-turtles—but black as widower's
weeds, heavy as chests of plate, with vast shells medallioned and orbed
like shields, and dented and blistered like shields that have breasted a
battle—shaggy too, here and there, with dark green moss, and slimy with
the spray of the sea. These mystic creatures, suddenly translated by night
from unutterable solitudes to our peopled deck, affected me in a manner
not easy to unfold. They seemed newly crawled forth from beneath the
foundations of the world. Yea, they seemed the identical tortoises whereon
the Hindoo plants this total sphere. With a lantern I inspected them
more closely. Such worshipful venerableness of aspect! Such furry greenness
mantling the rude peelings and healing the fissures of their shattered shells.
I no more saw three tortoises. They expanded—became transfigured.
I seemed to see three Roman Coliseums in magnificent decay.

Ye oldest inhabitants of this or any other isle, said I, pray give me the
freedom of your three-walled towns.

The great feeling inspired by these creatures was that of age: —
dateless, indefinite endurance. And, in fact, that any other creature can live
and breathe as long as the tortoise of the Encantadas, I will not readily
believe. Not to hint of their known capacity of sustaining life, while going
without food for an entire year, consider that impregnable armour
of their living mail. What other bodily being possesses such a citadel
wherein to resist the assaults of Time?

· · ·

As, lantern in hand, I scraped among the moss and beheld the ancient scars
of bruises, received in many a sullen fall among the marly mountains of
the isle—scars strangely widened, swollen, half obliterate, and yet distorted
like those sometimes found in the bark of very hoary trees—I seemed
an antiquary of a geologist, studying the bird tracks and ciphers upon the
exhumed slates trod by incredible creatures whose very ghosts are now defunct.

As I lay in my hammock that night, overhead I heard the slow weary
draggings of the three ponderous strangers along the encumbered deck.
Their stupidity or their resolution was so great that they never went aside
for any impediment. One ceased his movements altogether just before the
mid-watch. At sunrise I found him butted like a battering ram against the
immovable foot of the foremast, and still striving, tooth and nail, to force
the impossible passage. That these tortoises are the victims of a penal,
or malignant, or perhaps a downright diabolical enchanter, seems in nothing
more likely than in that strange infatuation of hopeless toil which so often
possesses them. I have known them in their journeyings to ram themselves
heroically against rocks and long abide there, nudging, wriggling, wedging,
in order to displace them, and so hold on their inflexible path. Their
crowning curse is their drudging impulse to straightforwardness in a
belittered world. . . .

Listening to these draggings and concussions, I thought me of the haunt
from which they came; an isle full of metallic ravines and gulches, sunk
bottomlessly into the hearts of splintered mountains, and covered for many
miles with inextricable thickets. I then pictured these three straightforward
monsters, century after century, writhing through the shades, grim as
blacksmiths; crawling so slowly and ponderously, that not only did toad-stools
and all fungous things grow beneath their feet, but a sooty moss sprouted
upon their backs. With them I often lost myself in volcanic mazes; brushed
away endless boughs of rotting thickets; till finally in a dream I found
myself sitting cross-legged upon the foremost, a Brahmin similarly mounted
upon either side, forming a tripod of foreheads which upheld the universal cope.

. . .

From a broken, stair-like base, washed, as the steps of a water-palace,
by the waves, the tower rose in entablatures of strata to a shaven summit.
These uniform layers which compose the mass form its most peculiar feature.
For at their lines of junction they project flatly into encircling shelves,
from top to bottom, rising one above another in graduated series. And as
the eaves of any old barn or abbey are alive with swallows, so were all these
rocky ledges with unnumbered sea-fowl. Eaves upon eaves, and nests upon
nests. Here and there were long birdlime streaks of a ghostly white staining
the tower from sea to air, readily accounting for its sail-like look afar.
All would have been bewitchingly quiescent, were it not for the demoniac
din created by the birds. Not only were the eaves rustling with them,
but they flew densely overhead, spreading themselves into a winged and
continually shifting canopy. The tower is the resort of aquatic birds for
hundreds of leagues around. To the north, to the east, to the west, stretches
nothing but eternal ocean; so that the man-of-war hawk coming from the
coasts of North America, Polynesia, or Peru, makes his first land at Rodondo.

. . .

Bird lime and rock, Buccaneer Cove, James Island

And yet though Rodondo be terra-firma, no landbird ever lighted on it. Fancy a red-robin or a canary there! What a falling into the hands of the Philistines, when the poor warbler should be surrounded by such locust-flights of strong bandit birds, with long bills cruel as daggers.

. . .

Male frigate bird displaying, Tower Island

I know not where one can better study the Natural History of strange sea-fowl than at Rodondo. It is the aviary of Ocean. Birds light here which never touched mast or tree; hermit-birds, which ever fly alone, cloud-birds, familiar with unpierced zones of air. . . .

As we still ascend from shelf to shelf we find the tenants of the tower serially disposed in order of their magnitude:—gannets, black and speckled haglets, jays, sea-hens, spermwhale-birds, gulls of all varieties:—thrones, princedoms, powers, dominating one above another in senatorial array; while sprinkled over all, like an ever-repeated fly in a great piece of broidery, the stormy petrel or Mother Cary's chicken sounds his continual challenge and alarm. That this mysterious humming-bird of ocean, which had it but brilliancy of hue might from its evanescent liveliness be almost called its butterfly, yet whose chirrup under the stern is ominous to mariners as to the peasant the death-tick sounding from behind the chimney-jam—should have its special haunt at the Encantadas, contributes in the seaman's mind not a little to their dreary spell.

. . .

The winged life clouding Rodondo on that well-remembered morning,
I saw had its full counterpart in the finny hosts which people the waters at its
base. Below the waterline, the rock seemed one honey-comb of grottoes,
affording labyrinthine lurking places for swarms of fairy fish. All were
strange; many exceedingly beautiful; and would have well graced the costliest
glass globes in which goldfish are kept for a show. Nothing was more striking
than the complete novelty of many individuals of this multitude. Here
hues were seen as yet unpainted, and figures which are unengraved.

. . .

Flamingos in crater lake, Bainbridge Island

It is known that burial in the ocean is a pure necessity of sea-faring life, and that it is only done when land is far astern, and not clearly visible from the bow. Hence, to vessels cruising in the vicinity of the Enchanted Isles, they afford a convenient Potter's Field. The interment over, some good-natured forecastle poet and artist seizes his paintbrush, and inscribes a doggerel epitaph. When after a long lapse of time, other good-natured seamen chance to come upon the spot, they usually make a table of the mound, and quaff a friendly can to the poor soul's repose.

As a specimen of these epitaphs take the following, found in a bleak gorge of Chatham Isle: —

"Oh Brother Jack, as you pass by,
As you are now, so once was I.
Just so game and just so gay,
But now, alack, they've stopped my pay.
No more I peep out of my blinkers,
Here I bee — tucked in with clinkers!"

—HERMAN MELVILLE

3. *SCIENTISTS*

CHARLES DARWIN

If there are indeed two sets of islands, the dream islands and the real, then Charles Darwin spent most of his time in the real. The other archipelago existed for him too, however. The Galápagos grew in his mind after he had left them just as miraculously as they grew in Melville's. They are magic islands. If we are to sanctify the desert mountains where Semitic prophets received their messages, then we should these desert islands where Darwin first heard his whisperings. What could be more mysterious and worthy of wonder than the lava hills on which man learned to see himself in a new image, and a God of a different face?

During the greater part of our stay of a week, the sky was cloudless,
and if the trade-wind failed for an hour, the heat became very oppressive.
On two days, the thermometer within the tent stood for some hours at 93°;
but in the open air, in the wind and sun, at only 85°. The sand was
extremely hot; the thermometer placed in some of a brown colour
immediately rose to 137°, and how much above that it would have risen,
I do not know, for it was not graduated any higher.

. . .

In the morning (17th) we landed on Chatham Island, which, like the others, rises with a tame and rounded outline, broken here and there by scattered hillocks, the remains of former craters. Nothing could be less inviting than the first appearance. A broken field of black basaltic lava, thrown into the most rugged waves, and crossed by great fissures, is every where covered by stunted, sun-burnt brushwood, which shows little signs of life. The dry and parched surface, being heated by the noonday sun, gave to the air a close and sultry feeling, like that from a stove: we fancied even that the bushes smelt unpleasantly.

. . .

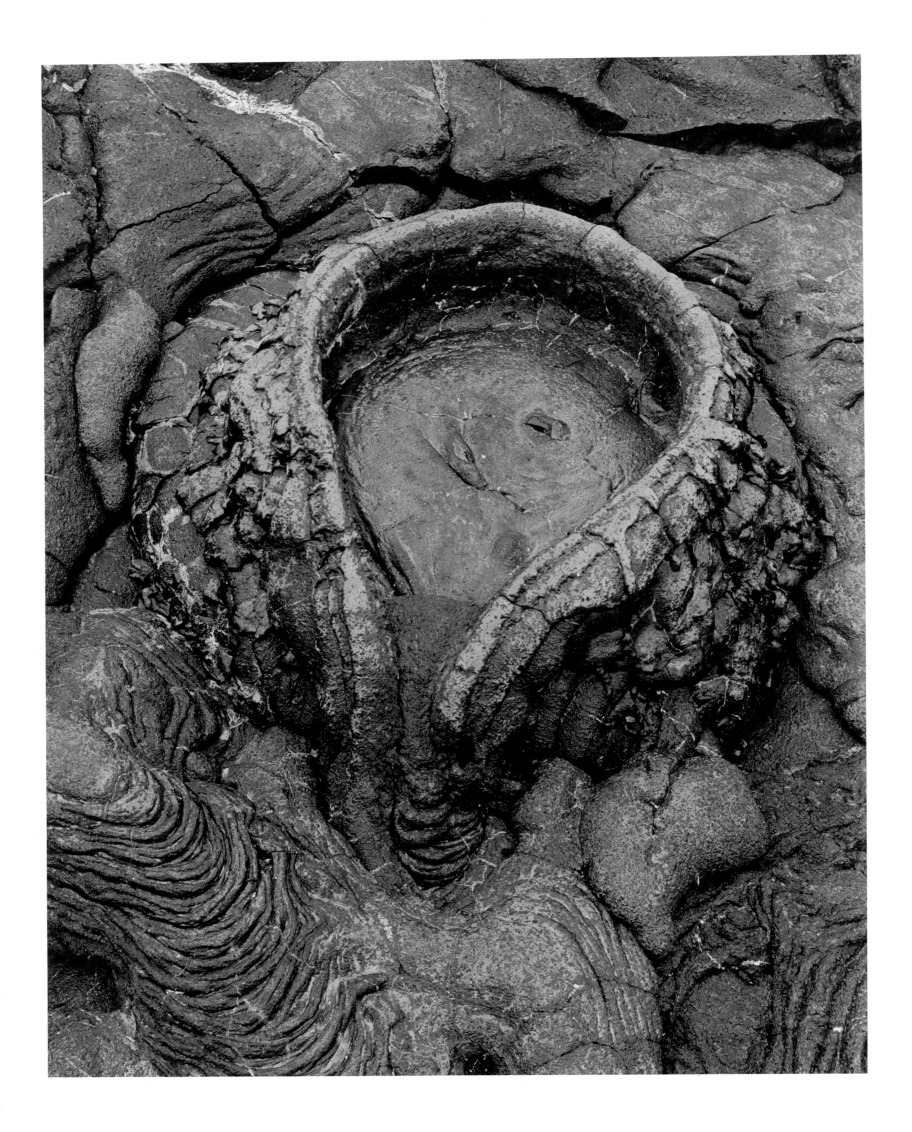

The *Beagle* sailed round Chatham Island, and anchored in several bays.
One night I slept on shore on a part of the island, where black truncated
cones were extraordinarily numerous: from one small eminence I counted
sixty of them, all surmounted by craters more or less perfect. The greater
number consisted merely of a ring of red scoriæ or slags, cemented together:
and their height above the plain of lava was not more than from fifty
to a hundred feet: none had been very lately active. The entire surface
of this part of the island seems to have been permeated, like a sieve, by the
subterranean vapours: here and there the lava, whilst soft, has been
blown into great bubbles; and in other parts, the tops of caverns similarly
formed have fallen in, leaving circular pits with steep sides. From the
regular form of the many craters, they gave to the country an artificial
appearance, which vividly reminded me of those parts of Staffordshire,
where the great iron-foundries are most numerous. The day was glowing hot,
and the scrambling over the rough surface and through the intricate thickets,
was very fatiguing; but I was well repaid by the strange Cyclopean scene.
As I was walking along I met two large tortoises, each of which must have
weighed at least two hundred pounds: one was eating a piece of cactus,
and as I approached, it stared at me and slowly stalked away; the other
gave a deep hiss, and drew in its head. These huge reptiles, surrounded by
the black lava, the leafless shrubs, and large cacti, seemed to my fancy
like some antediluvian animals. The few dull-coloured birds cared no more
for me, than they did for the great tortoises.

· · ·

The tortoise is very fond of water, drinking large quantities, and wallowing in the mud. The larger islands alone possess springs, and these are always situated towards the central parts, and at a considerable height. The tortoises, therefore, which frequent the lower districts, when thirsty, are obliged to travel from a long distance. Hence broad and well-beaten paths branch off in every direction from the wells down to the sea-coast; and the Spaniards by following them up, first discovered the watering-places. When I landed at Chatham Island, I could not imagine what animal travelled so methodically along well-chosen tracks. Near the springs it was a curious spectacle to behold many of these huge creatures, one set eagerly travelling onwards with outstretched necks, and another set returning, after having drunk their fill. When the tortoise arrives at the spring, quite regardless of any spectator, he buries his head in the water above his eyes, and greedily swallows great mouthfuls, at the rate of about ten in a minute. The inhabitants say each animal stays three or four days in the neighbourhood of the water, and then returns to the lower country; but they differed respecting the frequency of these visits. The animal probably regulates them according to the nature of the food on which it has lived. It is, however, certain, that tortoises can subsist even on those islands, where there is no other water than what falls during a few rainy days in the year.

. . .

The tortoises, when purposely moving towards any point, travel by night and day, and arrive at their journey's end much sooner than would be expected. The inhabitants, from observing marked individuals, consider that they travel a distance of about eight miles in two or three days. One large tortoise, which I watched, walked at the rate of sixty yards in ten minutes, that is 360 yards in the hour, or four miles a day, —allowing a little time for it to eat on the road. During the breeding season, when the male and female are together, the male utters a hoarse roar or bellowing, which, it is said, can be heard at the distance of more than a hundred yards. The female never uses her voice, and the male only at these times; so that when the people hear this noise, they know that the two are together. They were at this time (October) laying their eggs. The female, where the soil is sandy, deposits them together, and covers them up with sand; but where the ground is rocky she drops them indiscriminately in any hole: Mr. Bynoe found seven placed in a fissure. The egg is white and spherical; one which I measured was seven inches and three-eighths in circumference, and therefore larger than a hen's egg. The young tortoises, as soon as they are hatched, fall a prey in great numbers to the carrion-feeding buzzard. The old ones seem generally to die from accidents, as from falling down precipices: at least, several of the inhabitants told me, that they had never found one dead without some evident cause.

. . .

This archipelago, though standing in the Pacific Ocean, is zoologically part of America.

If this character were owing merely to immigrants from America, there would be little remarkable in it; but we see that a vast majority of all the land animals, and that more than half of the flowering plants, are aboriginal productions. It was most striking to be surrounded by new birds, new reptiles, new shells, new insects, new plants, and yet by innumerable trifling details of structure, and even by the tones of voice and plumage of the birds, to have the temperate plains of Patagonia, or the hot dry deserts of Northern Chile, vividly brought before my eyes. Why, on these small points of land, which within a late geological period must have been covered by the ocean, which are formed of basaltic lava, and therefore differ in geological character from the American continent, and which are placed under a peculiar climate,—why were their aboriginal inhabitants, associated, I may add, in different proportions both in kind and number from those on the continent, and therefore acting on each other in a different manner—why were they created on American types of organization?

. . .

The distribution of the tenants of this archipelago would not be nearly so wonderful, if, for instance, one island had a mocking-thrush, and a second island some other quite distinct genus; — if one island had its genus of lizard, and a second island another distinct genus, or none whatever; — or if the different islands were inhabited, not by representative species of the same genera of plants, but by totally different genera, as does to a certain extent hold good; for, to give one instance, a large berry-bearing tree at James Island has no representative species in Charles Island. But it is the circumstance, that several of the islands possess their own species of the tortoise, mocking-thrush, finches, and numerous plants, these species having the same general habits, occupying analogous situations, and obviously filling the same place in the natural economy of this archipelago, that strikes me with wonder. . . .

The only light which I can throw on this remarkable difference in the inhabitants of the different islands, is, that very strong currents of the sea running in a westerly and W.N.W. direction must separate, as far as transportal by the sea is concerned, the southern islands from the northern ones; and between these northern islands a strong N.W. current was observed, which must effectually separate James and Albemarle Islands. As the archipelago is free to a most remarkable degree from gales of wind, neither the birds, insects, nor lighter seeds, would be blown from island to island. And lastly, the profound depth of the ocean between the islands, and their apparently recent (in a geological sense) volcanic origin, render it highly unlikely that they were ever united; and this, probably, is a far more important consideration than any other, with respect to the geographical distribution of their inhabitants. Reviewing the facts here given, one is astonished at the amount of creative force, if such an expression may be used, displayed on these small, barren, and rocky islands.

. . .

The most curious fact is the perfect gradation in the size of the beaks
in the different species of Geospiza, from one as large as that of a hawfinch
to that of a chaffinch. . . . The beak of Cactornis is somewhat like that of a
starling; and that of the fourth sub-group, Camarhynchus, is slightly
parrot-shaped. Seeing this gradation and diversity of structure in one small,
intimately related group of birds, one might really fancy that from an
original paucity of birds in this archipelago, one species had been taken
and modified for different ends. In a like manner it might be fancied that
a bird originally a buzzard, had been induced here to undertake the office of
the carrion-feeding Polybori of the American continent.

—CHARLES DARWIN

What but the wolf's tooth whittled so fine
The fleet limbs of the antelope?
What but fear winged the birds, and hunger
Jewelled with such eyes the great goshawk's head?

—ROBINSON JEFFERS

Galápagos hawk, Punta Espinosa, Isabela Island

Marine iguanas, Punta Espinosa

JOSEPH SLEVIN

Life in the Islands is now easier for scientists than it was in the old days. After a week or two in the field, weary of the din of swallowtail gulls on Plaza Island, or of boobies on Tower, scratched by the thorns of Duncan or thirsty from a trip to Narborough, scientists can go home to Indefatigable Island and the Darwin Station. The laboratory is there for working on collections, and the living quarters, though small, are clean. Halfway down the road to the village is the Station bar. The scientists, when they are not working late by laboratory lights, walk to the bar in the evenings. If they are tired of their own company, as they often are, they can talk with Ecuadorians there, and drink Ecuadorian beer.

When their evening is over, there is the long walk home to the Station. The road is a white, sandy ribbon in the equatorial starlight. In places the dark water of the bay comes right up to the road and laps the rocks at its edge. Sometimes, as you approach these places, there is an invisible scurry and splash, a sea iguana retreating to a farther rock, deeper into the double shade of mangrove and equatorial night.

In 1905, when the California Academy of Sciences began its seventeen-month expedition to the Galápagos, there was no sandy road and no station. The only people on Indefatigable Island were ten shipwrecked sailors trying to survive on the coast. The scientists on the expeditions never knew about the sailors, and for them the island was uninhabited. Of the other islands, only three had small colonies.

The old photographs of the academy scientists look just like slightly older photographs of western American badmen. The scientists look as tough, though not quite so surly. They were men of science, but of a Western mold. They were more than cerebral; they had to be clever and sturdy as well. They carried tortoises from the far interiors of islands, across lava and through thorns, under a tropical sun, "backing them down," as whaling men had, over terrain that is nightmarish walking even when the walker is upright and unencumbered. They beached and repaired their boats, built pens and cages, hunted, fished, and navigated. Occasionally, when their supply of atoyas ran low, one of them would sail alone in their small sailboat to Albemarle, and then back again, twice across those notorious waters. They also made this trip for sulphur, mined from the volcano above Villamil, which they burned periodically in the sealed cabin of the *Academy* in an attempt to control the populations of flies, cockroaches and bedbugs there.

Joseph Slevin, herpetologist on the *Academy*, kept the journal by which we know the expedition. The journal comes alive, strangely, not when Slevin is discussing tortoises, iguanas, lava lizards, or the single Galápagos snake, but when he describes the quality of his life in the Islands. He was caught up in the adventure. The romance of the Islands, their pirate past and present disreputable characters, was what interested him. When he came to publish his piece on the Galápagos, it was not on Galápagos reptiles, but on the history of Galápagos exploration. There is a disproportionate number of sailing ships among the plates in his book; Slevin clearly had come to love their lines as much as those of geckoes or green turtles. It's a hint at the power of the Islands, that the herpetologist in him lost out to the Tom Sawyer.

Land iguana, Plaza Island

A large lagoon was found just back of the beach, surrounded by a growth of
mangroves and big trees. Tracks of wild cattle were all about the edges
and two tortoises were found half buried in the mud close to the bank.
Hunter, Nelson and Ochsner went hunting cattle and shot a large, red and
white bull. We had some of the meat for supper and wouldn't blame anyone
for being a vegetarian if they had no other meat than Albemarle bull.
Beck, King and myself went after tortoises and found several. They are not
rare in this particular locality. We skinned out one large male and packed
it down to the beach, so we could pick it up with the skiff as we pulled
back to the schooner. Making our way back to the landing, we got lost
in the mangrove swamp, and, as the tide was coming in, we had to make our
way through the tops of the trees. Finally arriving at the skiff, we found it
floundering about in the mangroves and half full of water. Nelson, Hunter,
Ochsner and Gifford had already left for the schooner. With the assistance
of Williams, we beached the skiff and dumped the water out. Making a
good getaway through the breakers, we reached the schooner shortly after
six o'clock, having left ashore the tortoise we had skinned in hopes that we
can pick it up in the morning. King is a little under the weather this evening,
having drunk too much water out of a mudhole near the lagoon. We heard
several wild dogs barking while we were ashore, but none came near
enough for us to see them. Quite warm now and nearly everybody is
sleeping on deck tonight.

. . .

Early in the morning Beck went ashore to interview the secretary and decided it best to go direct to Chatham as requested. We took the whole party on board the schooner: secretary, captain, interpreter and five soldiers. The latter made a fine looking army. One had an old French army hat about the vintage of 1880, some had no hats nor sandals, but were the proud possessors of undershirts and trousers, which seemed to be the uniform of the day. Their firearms were about the same period as the uniform hat and were old bolt-action rifles. One had a double-barrel shotgun, the firing pins of which were rusted fast. No ammunition at all was in evidence. No doubt it is too dangerous to let the soldiers get hold of any cartridges. However, what the army lacked, the commanding officer supplied. He was dressed in a light blue uniform of French design, with red epaulets, red stripe down his trousers, a huge red pompon on his hat, and a cavalry saber that, for size and polish, was the last word.

. . .

The General was found seated at his official desk, an old kitchen table with the drawer missing, attired in a white duck suit and a navy watch cap, probably donated by some sailor off of a visiting warship. He gave us some very powerful home brew to drink, and, when he observed the tears streaming down our cheeks, informed us that it may be a little strong for us, as we were not used to it. Personally I agreed with him, in that it was not only a little too strong but much too strong for any human being. After this, I took particular pains not to be included in any official visits. Even now, 25 years afterwards, whenever I think of General Plaza I can almost feel my insides on fire. The General seemed very much interested in our work when we informed him as to our plans and where we were from, etc. The interpreter then said: "The General says he can tell from your looks that you are gentlemen." This remark rather flattered us, as we had been out 110 days without a shave and only at our stop at Cocos Island had we fresh water to wash with.

. . .

Opuntias below Cerro Colorado, Santa Cruz Island

Our stock of whiskey in the medicine chest being somewhat depleted, Ochsner and I arose to the occasion, and, hurrying down below, got some clean alcohol out of a barrel, diluting it to about 75 per cent. A hurried trip to the galley was then made, and some juice bailed out of a dish of stewed prunes gave our home brew the desired coloring. After shaking well, we poured the concoction into a whiskey bottle. In less time than it takes to tell it, we had a drink that seemed to hit just the right spot, as the sailors drank it down in great gulps. The Governor made some queer facial contortions and seemed to think all was not well, as he declined a second drink, a thing never heard of in these latitudes. However, he was too polite to say anything and thanked us profusely.

—JOSEPH SLEVIN

WILLIAM BEEBE

No man but Darwin had more affect on the Galápagos, or was more affected by them, than William Beebe. His *Galápagos: World's End* caused widespread interest in the Islands and helped bring the first settlers to them. Beebe, like Melville, spent little time on the Islands, less than one hundred hours, but the hours were full enough for him to write his book on them. Where in Melville's imagination the Islands "expanded—became transfigured," in Beebe's it wasn't necessary that they do so. He was happy in the simple recollection of his six thousand minutes in the Galápagos, the minutes not as symbols, but for their sounds, smells and sights. Beebe had a wandering eye; he was interested in Galápagos history and inhabitants, in island vistas and colors and especially in island detail.

Isaac Newton once spoke of his seventeenth-century pleasure at picking up "a smoother pebble or a prettier shell than ordinary, whilst the great ocean of truth lay all undiscovered before me." Beebe as a scientist was perhaps born too late for this kind of research, but he did it anyway. His great talent was as beachcomber.

One of the most beautiful things in death is the giant thorny lobster
of the tropics. Each part of the great carapace and the sheaths of the legs,
the eye-stalks, the huge thorns and cornices of the head are marvels of
delicate carving and colour, and when death comes to this crustacean and the
fishes and the scavenger mollusks and worms have made away with all his
muscles and flesh, then the empty shell, as wonderful in carving as the
Taj Mahal, is washed up and pounded to pieces upon the lava, and all the
fragments scattered through the sand—a myriad mosaics of the most
exquisite sculpture and with pigments faded into unnamably delicate tones
and hues. As I casually unearthed some jewel of a leg-joint, well worthy
of a setting in platinum, a slender rod splashed with mauve and crimson,
with a galaxy of blue stars wound in a spiral about it, I realized more than
ever what a casual thing is man upon the earth. For untold ages since
thorny lobsters first crawled about in the waters of the upper chalk,
perhaps sixty million years ago, beautiful detritus such as this has littered
the tropical sands. Only by the merest accident had I stumbled upon it, and its
shape become beautiful in my brain, its pigment colour in my eye.

. . .

Worm, Floreana Island

During parts of the next two days I watched these birds (mockingbirds) and observed them most astonishingly to haunt the outer lava reefs within wave spray, and there to feed on flies and on small crabs and other crustaceans. And then I observed a thing of the greatest interest — the fact that very often the birds thus engaged teetered and tipped. All my life I have wondered why sandpipers went through this motion, every few seconds tipping up the whole body, as though it were hinged at the thighs. The head and neck rise and then the whole body bobs instantly forward, the tail rising in its turn. This habit gains in significance when we see the water-thrushes doing exactly the same thing — birds which are actually wood warblers, taken to a littoral life. The ouzels and smaller herons also bob, but less enthusiastically. Here were mockingbirds with a littoral habit developed probably only a short time ago, who occasionally teetered with their whole being in a fashion identical with that of the sandpipers. Two others of my party observed this very thing in mockers feeding along the edge of a land-locked lagoon. We have not the slightest clue as to the reason for this, it seems only in some strange way connected with a life of walking along shallow waters, whether mountain brook, millpond or the shore of the open sea.

· · ·

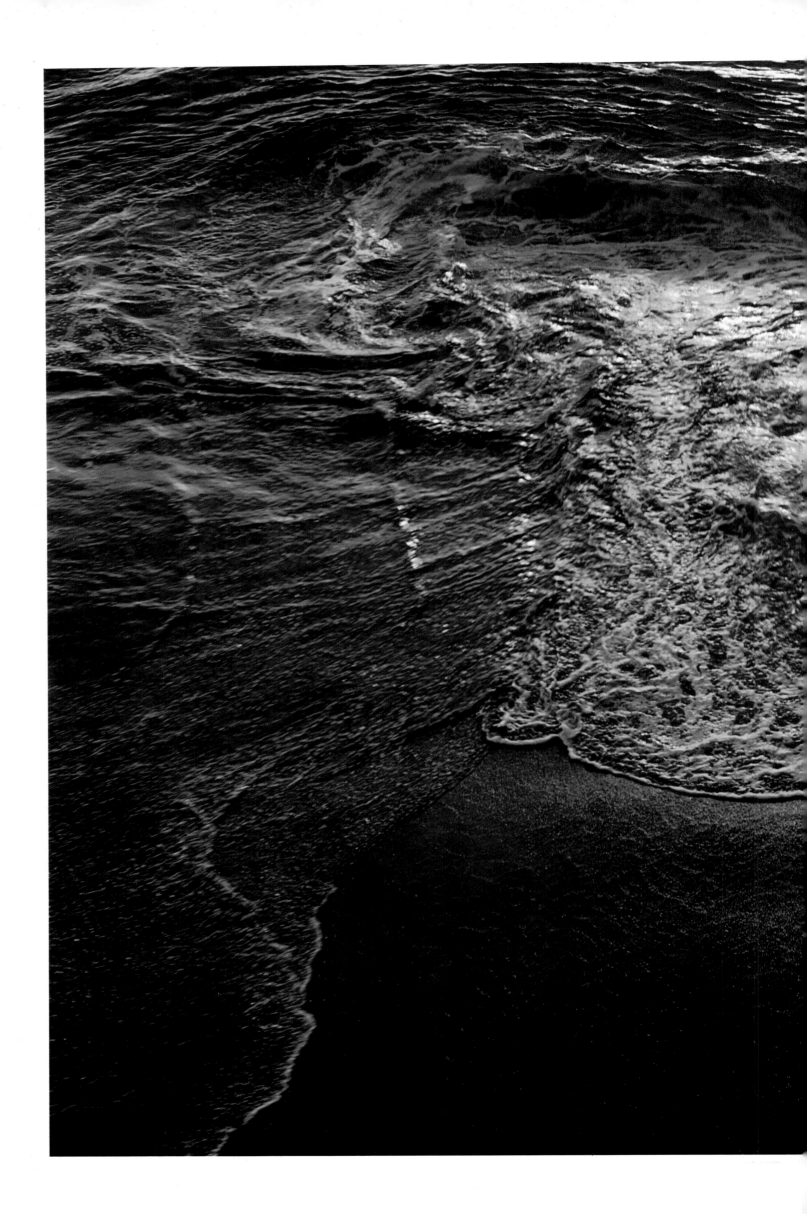

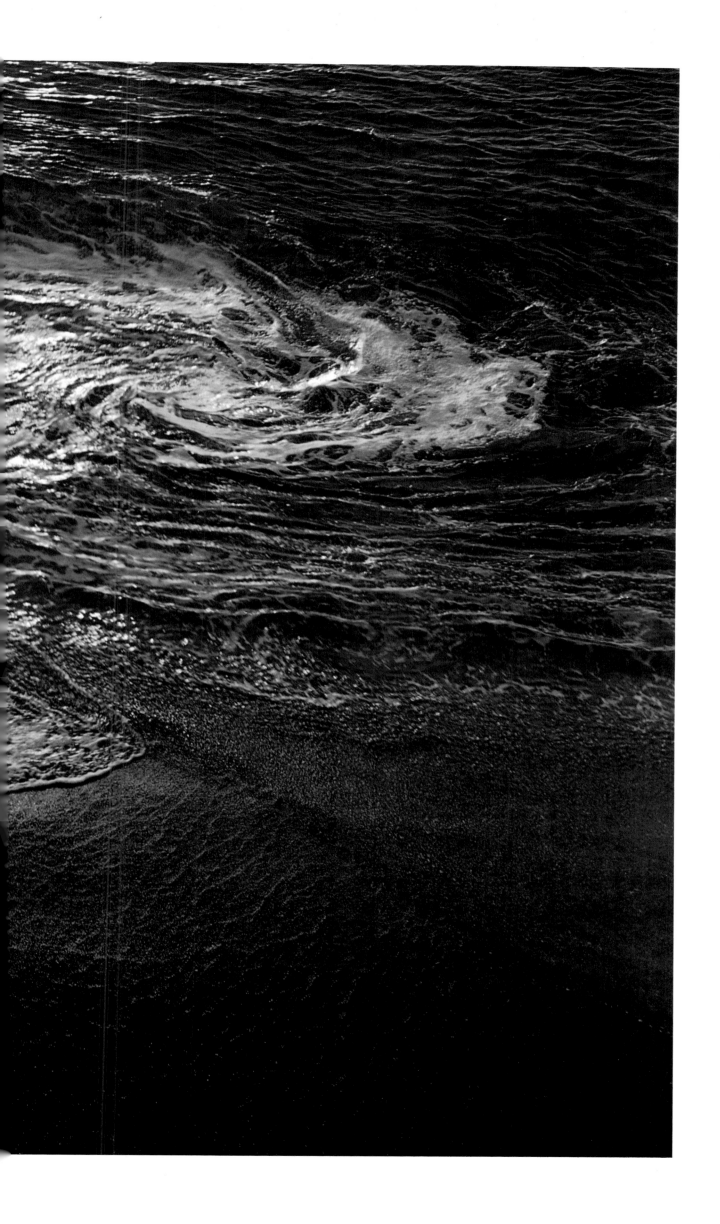

I left myself kneeling on the sand jealously scanning every inch. An
ingredient new to me was innumerable spines of club-spined sea-urchins —
millions upon millions of them, purple and yellow, apparently indestructible.
Later at Tower Island I found fork-tailed gulls making their nests of
several hundred of these short, stick-like structures, and one day on this
same beach I came across four of our sailors using them for poker chips,
so their utilitarianism is extremely catholic.

· · ·

Swallowtail gulls, Tower Island

Swirl in surf, Buccaneer Cove

Hosts of Sally Lightfoots were the most brilliant spots of colour above water in these islands, putting to shame the dull drab hues of the terrestrial organisms and hinting of the glories of colourful animal life beneath the surface of the sea. When such an outburst of crabs occurred as I have described, darting out of all possible and impossible cracks and crevices of the lava, they appeared to the imagination as organic reminders of the sparks and flames which once reddened these great beaches and these plains and mountains of lava.

. . .

The Bursera tree zone ended abruptly and I stepped on an out-jutting lava ledge, with an astounding view spread out before me. Down, down, down went the crater on all sides, and at the bottom hundreds of feet below was the floor—an enormous, round, flat area, dazzling white and dotted with what at this distance looked like a multitude of flies. My glasses showed them to be a host of nesting birds—big brownish white boobies. Not until some of my party walked out on the white sand did I realize the great size of Daphne's crater. They looked like beetles weaving over the surface. . . .

Here on this sunken crater floor, the young boobies during all the first months of their existence see only the dry lava and half-baked vegetation, and overhead the unbelievably blue sky. They probably have to remain a full three months or more before their wings are strong enough to carry them around and up, and if a booby has any imagination or ability to be surprised, with what emotion must he experience his first rise above the crater's rim, and see the ultramarine sea stretching away on all sides. Up to that time salt water has not existed for him, and the outside world has been represented only by passing clouds, the trips of his parents and the semidigested fish which he has plucked from the capacious throats of his mother and father.

Here and there were dead mummified remains of boobies. Among these I observed no very young birds, and only five adults, while all the rest were nearly grown young. The partly ossified skull was unmistakable even where the plumage had fallen off and blown away, and I believe that the crisis of the entire life is the achieving of the crater's rim.

. . .

I have spoken of the scattered dead birds, among which was a single, very ancient pelican—sole intruder of this blue-footed boobies' domain, which had been stricken in flight, as it passed overhead, or died after alighting. Under these dried corpses was a most interesting assemblage of insects and other arthropods. There were several species of beetles, but by far the most abundant were small, shiny black ones belonging to the same group as our familiar meal-worm beetles, which feed on our flour and cereals. The Daphne beetle is called *Stomion lævigatum*. The genus is found only in the Galápagos, and, like so many other creatures of this archipelago, is most closely related to a northern group.

This species has only been collected by Darwin, and from an unrecorded island. These beetles are evidently scavengers and scurry away from the light by dozens when the body of a dead booby is raised, or a loose stone overturned. The most interesting fact about them is the loss of the power of flight. Not only are the wings themselves abortive, but the elytra or wing coverts are soldered together. Yet here again we have considerable variation, and while in most individuals the elytra tear into small pieces, in others the suture between the once paired sides gives easily and the deeply concave cases rise and separate, a mockery, as there are no membrane organs of flight beneath. Here in the depths of this crater, these beetles have found no need to rise and whirr away to other haunts. The supply of dead bodies affords all that life could wish. They strive only to keep out of sight during the day-light when hungry lizards and finches are about.

· · ·

Dead booby and lava lizards, Daphne Crater floor.

Eyes, beak and feet were dull, but out of this sombreness, like fire out of
lava, billowed the burning scarlet of the enormous breast pouch.
When distended with air this was like a huge bladder, completely hiding
the bird. Its distension was not dependent upon conscious muscular action
for I saw birds quite sound asleep, with their beaks resting upon the top
of this balloon as if on a pneumatic pillow. They even soared with it
blown up, although in the wind they were put to constant effort in
balancing, compared with their pouchless fellows. The colour is at its best
when the sun is beyond the bird and shining through the skin tissue —
the scarlet being intensified, and colouring by reflection both the leaves
of the plant and the eye and feathers of the bird itself.

   I reached over and stroked it with but slight protest, the bird turning
away from me, but not snapping or pecking. Taking the tip of one great wing
in my hand I raised it up as high as I could reach. The bird spread the
other and, lightly as thistle-down, lifted and drifted away. Its ascent could
not have been more effortless had the pouch been filled with hydrogen.

. . .

Frigate birds, Tower Island

Fortunate is that bird or animal on the earth today which has found an
isolated niche for itself, where it may claim comparative sanctuary.
And this does not necessarily mean isolation from a geographical point
of view. It may be a gastronomic one, such as the scavenger vultures have
achieved, or the tough leaf diet of the hoatzin, feeding on substances which
are disdained by their fellows. Or it may be an isolation from fear of death
by daylight, such as is engendered in bats and goatsuckers; or from
actual low development of mentality as in the sloth; or an optical sanctuary
such as an insect which in color, form and movement strives ever to be
thought a leaf. But no more dramatic isolation exists than that of the
albatross, which, although furnished with legs and toes, yet for most of its
days spurns all solid earth and lives its life between sky and sea.

   When I first saw albatrosses at their breeding ground I experienced
a slight feeling of embarrassment, as if I were peeking through the blinds,
or looking behind the scenes. I feel much the same when, in the rotagravure
section of the Sunday paper, I see a photograph of some famous prima donna
making an apple pie in her kitchenette. The voice of a *chanteuse* and the
flight of an albatross are among the more wonderful things in the world,
so much so that at first we hesitate even to think of the authors in
relation to the trivial things of life.

. . .

I saw one coming in from the open sea, steadily as a triplane, without quiver or shift or balance of wing. When over the level ground the wings were tipped backward—the under surface presented as a brake, the legs lowered, the head held up, and with all its might the albatross bore back and began paddling furiously with its great webbed feet, seeking foothold as it taxied over the rough ground. Slower and slower became its speed, and finally the wings half reefed and gave up their power. But the feeling of land was too unaccustomed a thing—the bird sagged sidewise, tipped over a pebble, half fell across one of its fellows, and turned over, rolling undignifiedly several times before it quite stopped. Then it rose unsteadily, gathered itself together and looked around, clattering its beak and shaking its head, doubtless, saying to itself, that the land was not what it used to be.

I watched this bird and followed it for a considerable distance inland, but at its very first step I realized anew how far specialization for the air had gone. Flat feet, fallen arches, rheumatic joints, crippled limbs — all were suggested in its painful, appallingly awkward gait. At each step the entire body turned with the leg, and the whole head and neck swung around and down on the opposite side to aid in balance and in supreme endeavor for each succeeding step. I have never seen a more ungainly, effortful mode of progression, and when thrown on the motion picture screen it arouses as much amusement in an audience as the peripatetic progress of Charlie Chaplin. Some day an epic will be written on the law of compensation, the most dramatic thing in nature—the peacock with its aristocratic, incomparable display of exquisite colors, and its Billingsgate squawk of a voice; the nightingale, embodiment of glorious soul-stirring song, with feathers of dullest russet and grey. And here were albatrosses, master flyers, tottering miserably along as if each step brought acute agony.

Back of the headlands and all along the shore, somewhat removed from
the main mass of nesting birds, were the scattered albatrosses, probably
a thousand all told, two or three pairs close together, or a single bird
quite isolated. Some were casually resting, and these rose to their feet at my
approach and waddled slowly off. But most had already chosen their nesting
site and refused to leave either the bare eggless space upon which they
squatted, or the great oval shell which they kept so close beneath them.
The difference between the albatrosses and the other breeding birds,
in respect to my presence, was very striking. The former watched my
approach gravely and without fuss or sound chose their course of action.
If on an egg they permitted no familiarity, but snapped with their powerful
hooked beaks, and vigorously resented any advance. With a stick I gently
pushed one of the great birds back until the egg was uncovered, then took
it up, examined it, and replaced it, when the parent, with no show of
resentment or worry, shifted slowly forward, opened wide her breast feathers
and gently sank close down upon it again.

I am describing this rookery of albatrosses calmly, as if it was to me
merely an extension of the myriads of nests of the other seabirds. But in
reality it was one of the great experiences of my life, set apart from the rest
of the rookery as Buckingham Palace is from the houses of Grosvenor Square.
Here at last was the bit of dry land where these splendid creatures of the air
deigned to alight and to carry on the affairs of everyday life.

. . .

There is an authentic record of an invaluable, although it must be admitted involuntary, benefit rendered to man by an albatross. Some years ago there fell exhausted and dying from starvation upon the beach at Freemantle, West Australia, a great albatross. When found, it had a tin plate fastened around its neck on which was scratched the news of the wrecking of the French ship *Tamaris* three weeks before, and the survival of thirteen of her crew on Crozet Island. During this period the albatross had flown over four thousand miles of ocean, too terrified by its burden to stop to feed. It was a remarkable incident, quite reversing the experience of the ancient mariner;

> *"Instead of the cross, the Albatross*
> *About my neck was hung."*

Intellectually, man's relation with albatrosses has been less spectacular but of equal interest. Linnæus, one hundred and sixty-eight years ago, first played taxonomic Adam to the albatross, calling it *Diomedea exulans*. Its godfather was probably therefore the famous hero of the siege of Troy, but Grecian etymology provides a much more poetic and appropriate derivation, and it is pleasant to think of the albatross, whether winging over foam crests or at home on its little isle as being ever *Dio-medea* or God-counseled. In its specific appelation Linnæus was also happy for to the ordinary observer, the wandering albatross is truly *exulans*—homeless, banished apparently from all connection with solid land.

. . .

A chapter could almost be written about the names applied by sailors to the strange animals they met in their voyages. They are sometimes particularly interesting as reflecting the history of the time. So in Delano's *Narrative* we find a reference to the fact that in his day the sailors drew upon the Napoleonic wars in naming two of the denizens of the bird rookeries. The large solemn pelicans parading the barren shores were called the Russian Army, while the boobies, present in even larger numbers, received the name of Bonaparte's Army. The lovely snow-white bird, known to us as the tropic-bird, was then called the Boatswain's Mate, because of his clear, sweet whistle.

Delano wrote two excellent descriptions of the difference in manner of diving between the Russian Army and Bonaparte's Army. Concerning the pelican he says:

"They are the most clumsy bird that I ever saw. When in the act of diving they make the most awkward appearance that can be imagined; which cannot be better described than by comparing it to the manner in which a sailor washes his clothes, by making them fast to the end of a rope and throwing them from the forecastle into the sea; when they strike the water, they spread out, with the trowsers in one direction, the shirt in another and the jacket in a third."

. . .

Not a sound of night bird, or distant bark of dog in this desolate land;
only motionless heaps of cinders, piles of dust undisturbed by any breath
of air and mean foliage hanging limp and quiet as the rocks themselves.
Only once was the sight and sound of this oceanic isolation broken,
when one of the most brilliant meteors I have ever seen shot across the sky,
with a blazing glare of light and a low, sinister hiss, vanishing beyond
the distant crater rim as if it had plunged within—a worthy sanctuary for
this inorganic wanderer from outer space.

. . .

We were close enough to see every detail, but the fierce on-shore wind muffled every hiss and roar, every bubble and crash, and we might have been looking at the reproduction of some of the movies we were taking. From time to time, a huge portion of cliff would seemingly rise a little, tremble, and very slowly and gently topple forward, sending up a mountain of spray which alternately crashed in great breakers against the living and dead lava, and boiled and bubbled like some brobdignagian kettle.

It was astonishing to see a swell roll shoreward, curve up into a yellowish green wave, shatter against the scarlet lava and instantly rise and go floating off high in air toward the top of the distant mountain. It was a battle, a cosmic conflict among fire, water, earth and air such as only astronomers might dream of or a maker of worlds achieve.

Here at last was the very life blood of this Archipelago. Never would the black cliffs seem cold and meaningless again, but always memory would warm them and give them movement and color. Their twisted strands, their broken, porous bombs would seem to have cooled and exploded an instant before; every gas-made tunnel might redden and fill and pour at any moment.

· · ·

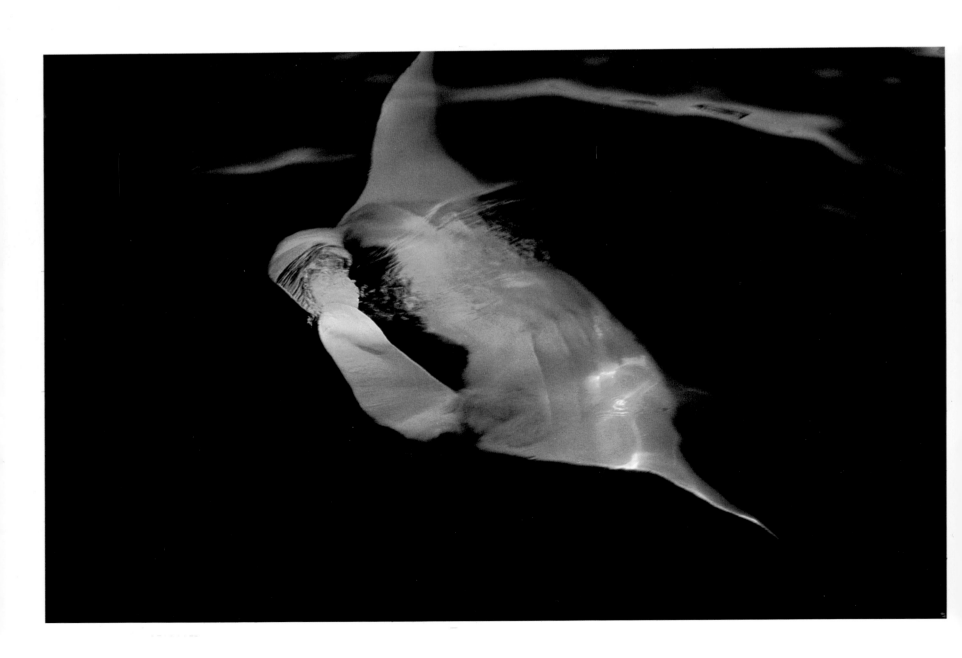

Once, when I was making my first flight in a plane, I had, for a short space of time, the soul-devastating sensation of being suspended motionless in the ether while the earth dropped away from me. That has never been repeated, but here on the bottom of the sea, looking upward at the great bubbles of breath, I can often conjure up the belief that I am actually looking at a constellation, a galaxy of worlds and stars, rolling majestically through the invisible ether. The background is as mysteriously colorless and formless as space itself must be, and as I peer out through my little rectangular windows I seem to be actually living an experience which only the genius of a Verne or a Wells can imagine into words. It suddenly flashes over me that in giving over my moon and stellar longings for the depths of the sea, I have in a manner achieved both.

I have even the sensations of a god, for in each of the spheres I have created, I see very distinctly my own image. But I also see many more interesting things and my moonings in the present instance were brought to an abrupt end by a glint of gold which appeared on each globule of air — a fiery pin-point which became an oval and soon a great spot as if a sun were rising behind me. If I were looking at a real planet such a thing might be a tremendous volcanic eruption on the surface. Twisting slightly and peering obliquely through my little periscope I saw what, after all, is the most joyous thing in life, an old friend in a new guise — another great golden grouper just behind me, revealed·by his reflected image on my ascending breath.

. . .

A turtle, almost as long as myself, swam into my ken. He was a much more satisfactory constellation than any in the heavens, of most of which I have never been able to make head or tail. But he was a turtle at its best. Until one has looked up and seen eight hundred pounds of sea turtle floating lightly as a thistledown overhead, balanced so exactly between bottom and surface that the slightest half-inch ripple of flipper motion was sufficient to turn the great mass partly over and send it ahead a yard — until then one has never really seen a turtle. Two years ago when I visited these islands, I watched the little penguins waddling about with their ever inimitable gait, I saw the cormorants awkwardly climbing over land, ever hauling themselves along by means of crooking their necks, the sea-lions unlovelily caterpillaring along the ground, and great hulks of turtles ploughing their way as much through as over the sand of the beaches. It was now my privilege to see these same creatures in their chosen element, graceful, glorified reincarnations of their terrestrial activities. In all of this I had no false illusions concerning my own relative functioning. While I have never heard any rumor as to my possessing any grace even at my best, yet on these same islands and beaches I can at least correlate my activity, and I can easily run down any of the creatures which I am discussing. Whereas here at the sea bottom I sprawl awkwardly, clutching at waving weeds to keep from being washed away by the gentle swell, peering out of a metal case infinitely more ugly than the turtle's head and superior to them only in my hearty admiration of their perfect coördination in an exquisitely adapted environment.

· · ·

Hardly a living thing was in sight. Two little moths fluttered about a flowerless, grey-green amaranthus, several ants appeared and waved their antennæ inquiringly in the direction of my gory limbs, and a great centipede crawled out of one crevice and into another. No movement of wind, no rustle of leaf, no voice of insect or bird troubled the vibrating waves of heat, or the sound of my pulse throbbing in my ears. Then just before I shifted, stretched and started back, a sulphur butterfly — most appropriately coloured for this particular bit of hell — drifted near, brushed against my face, rested its tattered wings on my knee for an instant, and fluttered on, headed where I could not follow — inland.

—WILLIAM BEEBE

Starfish, San Cristóbal Island

Cinder Cones and lava field, Sullivan Bay

The Islands are more comfortable now than they were in Slevin's and Beebe's day, but only in spots. The Station is there, and two more islands are inhabited, but otherwise the Galápagos are much as they were. The tradition of the ragged zoologist is still alive there.

On May 20, 1966, the yacht *Carybdis*, on its way south, put Dr. DeVries of the Darwin Station ashore on Barrington Island. It was not difficult, for he had only a black tin of food, marked *"Toda precaucion es poca,"* a tent, and four gerry cans of water.

DeVries was a Dutch ecologist hired by UNESCO to help run the Station and to do research work. He had chosen the birds of prey, the Galápagos hawks and owls, for his research. Barrington Island has many hawks, and he had come for that reason. The hawks are on Barrington in numbers because there are so many endemic rats there for them to feed on. On a previous trip to the island it had been necessary for DeVries to build a bonfire to keep the rats off. If the blanket of his cot touched the ground, he had to suffer their nibbling at his fingers and toes until the problem was corrected and his cot secured again. The rats were the reason that on this trip his food was in a tin.

DeVries was a large man, golden-brown from his months on the equator, and he was going bald. His face had an elfin look, accentuated by the small blond beard on his chin, and the effect was strange in a large man. His legs and forearms were crisscrossed with scars and healing cuts from the thorns of Duncan Island. He wore an old khaki shirt and some khaki shorts, both spattered very sparsely with rusty spots and stains. His black Ecuadorian tennis shoes had come untied and had unlaced themselves halfway down.

That night DeVries ate dinner aboard the yacht, his last dinner with humans for some time. Drinking his coffee, he looked up through the entranceway at the darkening sky and he stiffened. He had seen something outside, clearly, and a member of the crew asked him what it was. A Galápagos short-eared owl, DeVries answered. It could not have been more than an instant in the narrow strip of sky visible through that opening, but DeVries was so familiar with the silhouette that an instant's passage identified it.

DeVries slept that night on the yacht, though it rocked slightly on the lagoon and was cramped and surely less comfortable than his camp on the island. He would have the camp, and the island, enough to himself in the days to come. The next morning early the *Carybdis* sailed out of the lagoon, and DeVries was alone on a desert island in the middle of the blue Pacific.

SIERRA CLUB EXHIBIT FORMAT SERIES

Winner of the Carey-Thomas Award in 1964
  for the best achievement in creative publishing in the United States

EDITED BY DAVID BROWER

1. *This Is the American Earth,* by Ansel Adams and Nancy Newhall
2. *Words of the Earth,* by Cedric Wright
3. *These We Inherit: The Parklands of America,* by Ansel Adams
4. *"In Wildness is the Preservation of the World,"* by Eliot Porter
5. *The Place No One Knew: Glen Canyon on the Colorado,* by Eliot Porter
6. *The Last Redwoods: Photographs and Story of a Vanishing Scenic Resource,* by Philip Hyde and Francois Leydet
7. *Ansel Adams: A Biography. Volume I: The Eloquent Light,* by Nancy Newhall
8. *Time and the River Flowing: Grand Canyon,* by Francois Leydet
9. *Gentle Wilderness: The Sierra Nevada,* text from John Muir, photographs by Richard Kauffman
10. *Not Man Apart: Photographs of the Big Sur Coast,* with lines from Robinson Jeffers
11. *The Wild Cascades: Forgotten Parkland,* by Harvey Manning, with lines from Theodore Roethke
12. *Everest: The West Ridge,* by Thomas F. Hornbein, with photographs from the American Mount Everest Expedition
13. *Summer Islands: Penobscot Country,* by Eliot Porter
14. *Navajo Wildlands: As Long as the Rivers Shall Run,* photographs by Philip Hyde, text by Stephen Jett, edited by Kenneth Brower
15. *Kauai and the Park Country of Hawaii,* by Robert Wenkam edited by Kenneth Brower
16. *Glacier Bay: The Land and the Silence,* by Dave Bohn
17. *Baja California and the Geography of Hope,* photographs by Eliot Porter, text by Joseph Wood Krutch, edited by Kenneth Brower
18. *Central Park Country: A Tune Within Us,* photographs by Nancy and Retta Johnston, text by Mireille Johnston, introduction by Marianne Moore

THE EARTH'S WILD PLACES
within the Exhibit Format Series, a special series on
wildness around the world, published in cooperation with
The Conservation Foundation

19, 20. *Galapagos: The Flow of Wildness*
  1. *Discovery,* photographs by Eliot Porter, introduction by Loren Eiseley, with selections from Charles Darwin, Herman Melville, and others; and
  2. *Prospect,* photographs by Eliot Porter, introduction by John P. Milton, text by Eliot Porter and Kenneth Brower, both volumes edited by Kenneth Brower.